SECRETS OF AN ORGANIZED MOM

From the Overflowing Closets to
the Chaotic Play Areas: A Room-by-Room
Guide to Decluttering and Streamlining
Your Home for a Happier Family

BARBARA REICH

ATRIA PAPERBACK

NEW YORK   LONDON   TORONTO   SYDNEY   NEW DELHI

ATRIA PAPERBACK

A Division of Simon & Schuster, Inc.
1230 Avenue of the Americas
New York, NY 10020

First Atria Paperback edition April 2014

ATRIA PAPERBACK and colophon are trademarks of Simon & Schuster, Inc.

For information about special discounts for bulk purchases,
please contact Simon & Schuster Special Sales at 1-866-506-1949
or business@simonandschuster.com.

The Simon & Schuster Speakers Bureau can bring authors to your
live event. For more information or to book an event, contact the
Simon & Schuster Speakers Bureau at 1-866-248-3049 or
visit our website at www.simonspeakers.com.

Designed by Kyoko Watanabe

Manufactured in the United States of America

10   9   8   7   6   5   4   3

The Library of Congress has cataloged the hardcover edition as follows:

Reich, Barbara.
  Secrets of an organized mom : from the overflowing closets to the chaotic
play areas : a room-by-room guide to decluttering and streamlining your
home for a happier family / Barbara Reich.
     pages cm
1. House cleaning. 2. Orderliness. 3. Storage in the home. I. Title.
  TX324.R45 2013
    648'.5—dc23   2012026992

ISBN 978-1-4516-7285-5
ISBN 978-1-4516-7286-2 (pbk)
ISBN 978-1-4516-7287-9 (ebook)

Praise for Barbara Reich and

SECRETS OF AN
ORGANIZED MOM

"Reich delivers. Her book just might take the anxiety out of tasks that many find completely daunting and overwhelming."

—*Publishers Weekly*

"Every mom should read *Secrets of an Organized Mom*. Power-packed with all you need to know to get and stay organized, this book is the ultimate guide for anyone reorganizing, relocating, or just trying to make sense of the clutter."

—Tina Reber, *New York Times* bestselling author

"*Secrets of an Organized Mom* gets you excited to organize your home. Who knew that was possible? It is packed with great tips to help you create an organizing plan that's fast and effective . . . a huge relief for busy moms."

—MomItForward.com

"Barbara is a great editor. She took her razor sharp eye and cut a swath through my closet. When you can't see the forest through the trees, Barbara can. She's a true lifesaver!"

—Judith Regan, host of the *Judith Regan Show* on SiriusXM Stars

"Barbara Reich gives busy moms the tools to get their homes—and their lives—in perfect order. *Secrets of an Organized Mom* is full of helpful tips for tackling chaotic countertops, scary storage spaces, and everything in between. All hail the Clutter Queen!"

—ModernMom.com

"Barbara Reich makes having an organized house look so easy! And it can be if you follow her tips and stick with it."

—MacaroniKid.com

For my family, who provides me with a
steady stream of things to organize

CONTENTS

Contents

Contents

SECRETS OF AN
ORGANIZED MOM

INTRODUCTION

If you're a mom, no matter whether you're married or single, and no matter how involved your partner is, I guarantee that the lion's share of keeping the home together and functioning falls on your shoulders. I often joke that in my next life, I'd like to come back as my husband . . . married to me. I'm telling you, that man has a good deal. This is no insult to my husband or to anyone else's wonderful life partner—it's just a fact of life that moms tend to do more. And in my years of experience working with families, I've seen it's true whether the mother works outside the home or not. Taking care of our families is what we *do* as moms. It's in our nature, and we couldn't stop if we tried.

This doesn't mean that it's easy for us, however. And sometimes it seems to get harder every day. Our family's schedules are more chaotic, we have more stuff and more responsibilities. We have lists that get longer, never shorter, and we feel perpetually exhausted and burdened by how much we have to do and how little (we think) we actually get done.

Meanwhile, there are so many expectations of us. We're expected to nurture our children's developing brains, volunteer at school, keep our families healthy, our homes impeccably organized and decorated, our partners romantically satisfied, and our bodies well exercised. Oh, and we're also told to be sure to "take time for ourselves."

Most mothers I know feel like life is one big game of Whac-A-Mole. Just when we've smacked down one problem or responsibility, another one pokes up its stubborn little head. And we keep on flailing and reacting, doing our best, but with no time to formulate a plan of attack.

This book is your plan.

When I had my twins (who are now thirteen years old), I scaled back from full-time management consulting to part-time. I was used to commuting to an office for twelve-hour workdays, wearing power suits and heels. So it was a big transition for me. I loved being a mom and enjoyed meeting other parents, but often enough I'd find myself getting a little antsy on playdates. I'd look around for something to do, and I'd end up organizing the toys and straightening the shelves.

You can quickly gain a reputation for yourself by doing that. So when a friend of mine heard of someone who needed help setting up a home office, she suggested that he hire me. And no, she didn't ask me first. Bless her, though, that first referral quickly multiplied into more, and before long I had a business that I love.

The truth is that the seeds for my home organizing business were planted long before that. I was born to organize, but it wasn't until I turned eight that my talents were recognized by others. That year marked a life-changing turning point for me. Twice in one twelve-month period I was publicly acknowledged for being a neat freak. And by acknowledged, I mean *rewarded*. It was heady, that praise. It was addictive. It was like the first smattering of applause for the wannabe star in the grammar school play. After that, it's Hollywood or bust. For me, a career as a professional organizer became my destiny.

I grew up in South Florida, the land of sunshine, beaches, and chain stores. The biggest grocery chain was Publix, and they were always having some kind of contest or promotion. So when they advertised a coloring contest, I decided to enter. Each contestant was given an intricate design with a circus motif and lots of tiny details to fill in with color. I sat down, and I didn't stop coloring that piece of paper until every single square centimeter was filled in.

I can still remember the phone ringing one afternoon and my mother saying to me, "Barbara, you have a phone call." I could tell from her tone of voice that it was something important. I held the receiver tentatively, nervously, and an adult voice on the other end told me that I had won the Publix coloring contest. And the prize? A ticket for me and one adult to see the Ringling Bros. and Barnum & Bailey Circus—and to meet the world-famous lion tamer Gunther Gebel-Williams. Not only that, but I'd get to take an afternoon off from school because they weren't about to give us free tickets to a weekend show.

It shouldn't have surprised me that I won the contest. I had to be the only child who not only colored entirely within the lines but also made sure every single crayon stroke went in the same direction. If I made a mistake, I peeled off the wax with my fingernails or meticulously covered my error with white crayon. It was a masterwork of single-minded devotion to detail. How could I lose?

If winning weren't enough positive reinforcement, imagine my preadolescent joy when the platinum-blond and shirtless Gunther Gebel-Williams pulled up in front of my front-row seat and invited me to take a ride around the center ring in his horse-pulled cart. The crowd, the lights, the cheers. More important: Gunther Gebel-Williams's tight white bell-bottoms and perma-tan. This was potent stuff for an eight-year-old girl.

If my first reward for neatness was all about romance, my second was all about terror. My parents sent me to a summer camp that I adored beyond all reason. It was called Camp Universe, and it was perched next to the shimmering waters of Lake Miona in Wildwood,

Florida. I look back on my time there and wonder a bit if my parents didn't misread the pamphlet and ship me off to boot camp instead of summer camp. We were constantly being lined up to do something—in size order from shortest to tallest. And our cabin would lose points if our line weren't perfectly straight.

Right before visiting day, the camp would conduct what was called the Moss Hunt. Remember, this was Florida, so moss grew everywhere. But rather than hire people to clean it up, the camp came up with the brilliant idea of making it an activity for the campers. I'm telling you: This wasn't summer camp, it was a chain gang. We'd be out in the blazing heat and humidity, picking up piles of moss (Spanish was the most valuable find, because it was the rarest) and stacking it in heaps for removal. The camp staff would measure each cabin's piles, and the cabin with the tallest piles got the most points. In addition to moss, there was an elaborate system of points for all the gum and candy wrappers, bottle tops, and beer bottle caps we could find. My cabin always won the competition, thanks to my zeal for the job.

I loved that camp to a bizarre and possibly pathological degree. I loved all the order. And I really loved laundry day. There was no better feeling for me than when all my clothes were clean *at the same time.* I loved to refold each item and put it in its proper space in my cubby. I loved making hospital corners on my bunk bed.

My moment of triumph occurred during Camp Color War. It made sense that a camp as army-like as this one would have a cabin neatness event. I remember my beating heart as every girl in my cabin stood at attention in front of our beds and cubbies, waiting to be inspected by scary Dan, the camp director with the shiny whistle around his neck and the clipboard that seemed permanently attached to his hand. He stopped in front of my bunk, flanked by the captains of the gold and the blue teams, and he scanned my bunk and my cubbies up and down, then down and up. He lingered, I perspired. Was something not arranged at a perfect right angle? I resisted the temptation to turn around and look, because I'd get points off for not standing at attention (of course).

Then scary Dan said, "Whose cubby is this?"

"Mine, sir," I squeaked.

He nodded. "Extra points for the blue team."

I have to tell you: even the obvious appeal of Gunther Gebel-Williams's well-oiled chest was no match for the relief of a cabin full of eight-year-old girls standing at attention.

We're often given two seemingly conflicting pieces of advice. One group of people tells us to follow our heart. The other tells us to be practical. Luckily for me, the two don't conflict. There are few things that give me greater joy than practicality. And I like to think that I communicate my joy to the clients who hire me to help organize their homes.

If I had to come up with the biggest roadblock between most women (especially moms) and their desire for organization, it's that a whole industry is conspiring to make it all seem so complicated and unattainable. We're surrounded by images of what the perfect home looks like—and usually, it's a catalog picture in which the hangers are all spaced three inches apart and the clothing inside is all white or tan. I don't know about you, but my closet doesn't look like that. No one's clothes are only two colors, and no one has only ten articles of clothing.

Because there's such a wide gulf between fantasy and reality when it comes to home organization, a lot of the moms I've met over the years throw in the towel. Their email inboxes are filled to capacity, and their closets, attics, basements, garages, and storage areas are stuffed to the gills with all the items that they a) don't know how to get rid of or b) don't know how to organize in such a way that those things are accessible and therefore usable. These moms get understandably panicked every time they miss a birthday, are assessed a credit card late fee, or look for an outfit to wear to work. Or maybe they think they're doing fine until that second, or third, or fourth baby comes along and everything suddenly becomes unmanageable.

There is a happy middle ground between fantasy and chaos, and that's where most of us want to live. My goal with my clients isn't to make them perfect or even to make them more like me. Even my husband thinks I'm crazy, and he's a really neat guy. I'm so crazy that back when I was working in an office, my coworkers thought it would be hilarious to move my stapler one inch to the left and then wait to see if I'd notice. P.S., I noticed. It doesn't bother me, though. I'm content with my predilection for order. But I don't require everyone to twitch like I do when the office supplies are rearranged.

The world is full of all kinds of wonderful people, and chances are, your family members range from the neatest to the most organization-ally challenged. That's okay. The key is that your home works for you and everyone in it. I guarantee that a messy, disorganized home works for *no one.* Those people who gesture to their piles and say, "Oh, but I know where everything is"? Don't believe them.

I'll tell you what often happens, and I bet this describes you at one stage or another: There's one area of your home that is disorganized or, more likely, there are multiple. The disorder is starting to drive you nuts, and although you've complained to the rest of the family about it, their response is to shrug or to turn up the volume on their iPods. So you go out and buy a bunch of storage containers, and you hope that the containers themselves will organize you.

You spend a lot of money, and you bring home all the contain-ers, and maybe you even put a lot of stuff in them, which seems like progress because at least now you can't see all the stuff that is making you feel disorganized. In truth, you haven't made any progress at all, because you haven't come up with a simple system that works for *you,* and therefore you haven't given yourself or the rest of your family the guidelines needed to help *maintain* the system.

Disorder reigns again, you vow never to buy another container, and you decide that you aren't an organized person. Such resignation doesn't help you in the long run, because the ongoing messiness of your life creates a constant low- (and sometimes high-) level feeling of anxiety in your household. You know you don't want to live like this, and you suspect that your family doesn't, either.

This is where I come in. I'm based in New York City, where even my wealthiest clients have space issues. I've been in multimillion-dollar homes with atrocious-looking closets. *Everyone* has messes, whether the mess is in the back of a walk-in closet or in the corner of the living room. Some of us have the luxury of a little more space, and some of us have barely enough to turn around in. We all need to work with the space we have. And when economic times are tough, it becomes even more urgent for us to find ways to be content with what we currently have—whether that's the square footage under our feet or the clothing hanging in our closets.

My clients (almost all of them moms) call me in when they've tried to organize things themselves but they've given up because they don't know where to begin. I visit all of my clients personally. I sit down with them at their computers and go through their emails, and I press the delete button—over and over and over again. I tell them what to keep, what to toss, what to file. I get down on the floor in their playrooms and up on a stepladder in their closets, and I don't hesitate to grab the Clorox wipes and clean the shelves of accumulated layers of dust. It's not glamorous work—even in the most glamorous homes—but it's tremendously satisfying. In a few short hours, I can transform a front hall closet in a way that enables every member of the household to get out of the home on time in the morning—and if that isn't an improvement to quality of life, I don't know what is.

As a married mother of twins, not to mention someone who has been in the farthest recesses of countless homes, I know all the trouble areas. Better yet, I have the solutions. My advice applies no matter what your household circumstances—whether you live in an apartment or a house, in the city, country, or suburbs, and whether you have one child or multiple. The lessons here also work no matter whom you live with—whether you're blessed with a neat freak like me or a spouse who barks at you if you even think about recycling that six-month-old issue of the *New Yorker*.

Whatever organizational nightmare makes you crazy on a daily basis, the antidote can be found here—from dealing with your home office filing (ugh) to that box of photos you keep meaning to stick in an album, to figuring out what to do with the things you don't want and don't need but can't seem to get rid of (sound familiar?). No stone goes unturned, from your front door to the deepest recesses of your computer and your storage areas.

Most important, this book shows how every member of your family can breathe easier, live happier, hang up their own coats, find the Advil, use the milk before it spoils, and maybe even open a closet without grimacing or covering their eyes. Doesn't that sound nice?

1

THE BASICS
Some Truly Simple Ground Rules

Despite the fact that I am filling this book with a lot of words about organizing, I don't do a lot of talking on my client visits. When I arrive at the door, the last thing clients need is to be lectured on organization. They're usually desperate by that point, and I want to show them right away how quickly they can feel a little more in control. Also, I find that most people learn better by seeing and doing.

My clients' time is precious, and yours is, too. So let's dig in. The first order of business is to **identify your home's "hot spot."**

A hot spot is the area that drives you absolutely the craziest. It could be a closet or a whole room. Either way, it weighs you down psychologically and slows you down physically. If you find that your search for a single hot spot in your home is turning into a laundry list of hot spots, then stop a moment and take a breath. Look at the list again. For sure, there is one thing that gives you greater anxiety than any other. That is your hot spot, and that is what you are going orga-nize first. And if the very idea freaks you out, then you know you've chosen the right one. Meanwhile, don't throw away the list—after you complete the most important task, you can gradually work your way through the rest.

The next requirement is to **open up your calendar and schedule the time to tackle your hot spot.** Then make that time as sacred as if you had a paid organizer looking over your shoulder. In my experi-ence, two hours is the right block of time to devote to each hot spot. Much more than that can be too tiring and overwhelming; less than that really isn't enough time to make an impact. A few minutes of or-ganization here or there isn't going to scratch the surface, and by the time you return to the task a few days (or weeks) later, what little you cleared away has already been filled with more stuff.

Because I want you to work in order of the areas that are highest priority to you, feel free to skip around in this book. If the office is your albatross, then don't hesitate to go straight to chapter 10. If your chil-dren's toy accumulation is driving you nuts, then off you go to chap-ter 4. The beauty of my system is that once you learn it, you can apply it to any situation. Therefore, expect some repetition of rules and ad-vice, whether you're bringing order to the kitchen or the bathroom or the closet. By the end of this book, you'll feel like you could organize *anything* just by following the same basic principles. But don't run off quite yet—first you need to learn the basics.

The Four-Step Method

No matter what area of the home you're organizing, my basic method for tackling the job is the same. You'll see this method in each chapter, and you can apply it to something as small as a drawer or as large as a room. Here are the four basic steps:

1. **Purge.** You can't be organized if you have too much stuff. This is why the first priority is to get rid of what's broken, unneeded, unworn, unloved, and otherwise cluttering your space.
2. **Design.** It's time to create the infrastructure you need, from drawer dividers to shelves and filing cabinets.
3. **Organize.** This is the fun part: Now that there's a place for everything, we get to put everything in its place.
4. **Maintain.** There's no point in getting organized if you can't stay that way, so the final step is to devise the systems that will keep you on track for the long term.

The Ten Commandments of Organizing

Let's set a few ground rules that apply to any home, no matter the size. Consider these my Ten Commandments of Organizing:

1. **Do the thing that is most distasteful to you first.** We already know how this wisdom applies to homework and paying the bills, and it works for organizing as well. If your desk makes you ill every time you look at it, then clean your desk. If you tackle the thing you hate first, your anxiety level will drop exponentially, and your quality of life will soar.

2. **Routines work.** Do it the same way every time. Put your purse in the same place, your phone in the same pocket within your

purse, and charge your phone next to your purse in the same place every night. It's the foolproof way of never again misplacing anything.

3. **Freebies are not your friends.** As far as I'm concerned, there are almost no freebies that are useful. Unless it's a free sample of a product that you already use, then anything you get for free is something that you wouldn't have bought yourself. Therefore, it's unlikely to be something that you will ever use, and it will inevitably take up space in your home until the day when you get around to throwing it in the trash. This rule goes for free tote bags, gifts with purchase, water bottles, mugs, and T-shirts. Do you really want to walk around town advertising the merits of your bank?

4. **Beware of junk mail.** Did you ask for the catalog that just arrived? No. So why would you give it a precious spot on your coffee table or in your entryway? And if you did ask for that catalog, then stop doing that, please! There is nothing in a catalog that you can't find online, and catalogs encourage less thoughtful, less intentional shopping. Catalogs are lose-lose-lose. They take up space, they're bad for the environment, and they encourage unnecessary spending. In short, catalogs are the enemy. The same thing goes for all other varieties of junk mail (credit card solicitations, etc.). Directly into the recycling bin they go.

5. **Store like with like, and designate a place for everything.** I can't tell you how many homes have batteries in multiple places, lightbulbs tucked away in various drawers, drawing pads in multiple rooms—you get the idea. Keep lightbulbs with lightbulbs so that when a light goes out, you know exactly

where to look for a replacement bulb (and you know when you need to buy more). Having multiple storage locations is a recipe for frustration and breeds a chaotic environment.

6. **Store things where you use them.** You'd be surprised how few of us do this. For instance, in many households, the daughter's hair is combed and braided at the breakfast table because we're all multitasking in the morning. So why would you keep the brush and ponytail holders in a drawer in the bathroom? Instead, keep these items in a plastic container (or tucked in their own drawer) in the room where you use them. The same goes for your makeup, your children's art supplies, etc.

7. **Get it off the floor.** The floor is not a storage option. Avoid having any boxes, bags, or toys that reside there permanently.

8. **Ignore sunk costs.** The original price of an item is not nearly as relevant as whether you use it, will ever use it, and how much space it occupies in your home and in your mind. When deciding whether to get rid of something, don't think about how much you paid for it—think only about whether you like having it around.

9. **Use one kind of hanger, storage container, etc.** This is a simple remedy to what I call "visual clutter"—that feeling of anxiety when everything is a jumble and your eye doesn't know where to go. Clothes hang better and more uniformly if they are all on the same kind of hanger. Moreover, your view of your clothing is made simpler and more calming if your hangers are all the same color. It doesn't matter what kind of hanger you choose, just make sure they are all the same. This goes for

storage containers as well. If all your containers are uniform in style and color, they will be easier to stack, and the visuals will be much more pleasing.

10. **Make a decision and act on it.** This is the biggie—I saved the best for last. If you receive an invitation, respond yes or no. Don't look at it, ponder it, then put it in a stack. Don't look at it again in two days and then reshuffle that growing stack. The fact is, if you're ambivalent, you probably don't want to go, right? The same thing goes for unwanted items in your house. If you hate that lamp, why would you store it in your closet? Don't delay making a decision: You hate it, so get rid of it.

The Tools of Organizing

As I've already stressed, my approach to organizing is all about simplicity. I don't believe that good organization requires purchasing a ton of supplies. The whole goal of being organized should be having less stuff, not more.

One of the major side benefits of being organized is that you save money when you're not purchasing unnecessary or duplicate items. I feel the same way about the organizing tools that I recommend to my clients. Simple is best, and these items don't have to be expensive. I don't care what brand you buy—it's much more important to me that the items are **uniform, usable, and take up the right amount of space.** You don't need a lot of specialized items for every room of the house. In fact, many of my favorite items can be used in almost any room or closet. Finally, while purchasing these items involves some initial expense, I guarantee that the years of satisfaction and usefulness they'll provide will be well worth the price.

Here are a few general guidelines for items I strongly recommend, as well as a few things to avoid.

RECOMMENDED:

☐ **Automatic labeler.** My passion for this organizing tool cannot be overstated. Get your box of stuff that you've created after storing like with like, stick a printed label on it ("lightbulbs," for example), and suddenly, like magic, order is brought to chaos.

☐ **Clear plastic containers with drawers.** I call these the "little black dresses of organizing" because they're so versatile. They're particularly great for children's art supplies and smaller toys, and they can be just as effective for toiletries, travel supplies, you name it. They can be stacked on a bookshelf in a child's bedroom, and if the child wants the one with crayons, he can pull out the drawer and then return it when he's finished. If the drawers are clear, he can see crayons inside. If the drawer is also labeled, he can read that there are crayons inside, which is a little bonus for those budding young readers. Genius.

☐ **Plastic containers with lids.** These boxes are best for under-bed storage (out-of-season clothes, wrapping paper) or upper-level storage for items that you don't retrieve often (holiday decorations). You can stack them, which maximizes your storage. If the containers are all the same style and in the same color, they will look neater and more organized. Moreover, if they're labeled, then you'll never again have to wonder what the heck is in that box at the top of the closet.

☐ **Bins.** Open-topped storage is best for items that are retrieved often, especially by young children, who will find tops cumbersome. Even adults can find a lid annoying when they need something in a hurry. Bins are particularly great for organizing hats, scarves, and gloves in closets; they can also be good for pet supplies and toys.

☐ **Coated cardboard boxes with lids.** Also called art files or document boxes, these are the best system ever invented for storing your children's artwork and memorabilia. More on this in Chapter 11.

☐ **Decorative containers.** No one wants a sea of plastic in the living room, so in public spaces, your choice of boxes and bins should lean more toward something that fits your decor, whether wicker, fabric-covered, wood, or whatever else pleases you. Just remember Commandment 9, and make sure they all match.

☐ **Trays.** These can be found at any price point to fit any decor, and they are the perfect way of bringing intentional order to a collection of items that might have seemed random otherwise. Whether used on a desk to corral a dish of paper clips, a stapler, and some Post-its, or on a kitchen counter to hold a pepper grinder, dish of garlic, and some vinegar, they're a miraculous organizing tool. Plus, my clients are relieved when I tell them that not everything has to be hidden away in a drawer or storage container.

NOT RECOMMENDED:

✄ **Containers that are too big.** When we have a lot of stuff to store, our tendency is to buy the biggest boxes or containers available. However, that encourages us to keep too much and also to put potentially unrelated items in the same container. Under-bed and out-of-season clothing storage can be on the larger side, but you don't want extra-large and unwieldy storage containers in your closet—and certainly not on an upper shelf, where they'd be hazardous to retrieve.

✂ **Mismatched containers.** No matter how attractive they are individually, these are a no-no. In homes where there have been several attempts to get organized over the years, it's common to find all different kinds of containers in various styles. It's better to have some containers than none at all, but over time, and as budgets allow, I encourage my clients to divest themselves of what's unmatched—not just because it doesn't look great but because it cuts down on storage space when boxes don't stack neatly.

Deciding to Donate, Recycle, or Throw Away

It's not all that difficult to figure out what you need to get rid of. Every item in your home can be put to the same test, whether it's clothing or a tablecloth or a piece of furniture. I call it the Barbara Reich Eliminating-Clutter Quiz:

1. Is the item in good condition and/or can it be repaired?

   If the answer is NO, out it goes.

   Hint: If it's broken, then fix it. If it can't be fixed, then get rid of it.

2. Have I used it/worn it in the last year?

   If the answer is NO, out it goes.

   Hint: Past behavior is the best indicator of future behavior. If you haven't had occasion to use it or wear it in a full year of normal activity, out it should go.

3. Will I ever use it/wear it again?

   If the answer is NO, out it goes.

   Hint: You squeaked through the last question by telling yourself that the item might come in handy at some point in the future. But really, how likely is that set of circumstances ever to occur?

4. Am I holding on to it because someone I love gave it to me but I hate it?

   If the answer is YES, out it goes.

   Hint: If you don't like it because it doesn't suit your taste or lifestyle, why are you keeping it? It's not doing anyone any good stuffed in your closet or begrudgingly dragged out for show once a year.

5. Is it justifying the space it's taking up?

   If the answer is NO, out it goes.

   Hint: If the item is large and used rarely, do you need to use it at all? And on those very seldom occasions when you might need such an item (whether it's skis or folding chairs), can it be rented or borrowed?

6. If I discarded it and found I needed it later, is it replaceable?

   If the answer is YES, then get rid of it.

   Hint: This applies to all those items that seem practical—spare extension cords, fans, umbrellas, bags, etc.—but aren't used. If you don't currently need them and they're highly replaceable, then ask yourself: Isn't your space much more precious than that item?

One you've realized how much you can get rid of, you have to figure out how best to dispose of all that stuff. My clients can get positively gleeful once they start filling trash bags—it's such a relief to get rid of all that junk, they practically skip to the curb while carrying them out. But it's true that all those bags of garbage can look mighty wasteful from an environmental perspective.

I encourage my clients to donate as many of their unwanted items as possible. I also rail against bringing so much stuff into our homes in the first place. (I've threatened to cancel some of my shopaholic clients' credit cards.) We're all guilty of buying too much food we don't eat, too many clothes we don't wear, and too many toiletries we don't use. It's time to put an end to that. If you follow the advice in this book, you won't just be more organized, you'll also save money, *and* you'll be doing your part to save the earth.

Of course, plans for the future don't address what to do with the current mess in your storage unit or basement or closet. For that, you need some guidelines:

- **Paper** can be recycled, and that goes for everything from documents to school papers to magazines—confidential documents can be shredded and then recycled.

- **Electronics** are trickier. If the item is broken or outdated to the point that donation isn't possible, then the next best alternative is to locate a nearby safe-disposal program, which should be a computer search away. In some locations, such as New York City, the trashing of certain electronics will be banned in the near future. As more communities move in that direction, finding disposal programs will become easier.

- **Clothing** must be clean and in good condition in order to be acceptable for donation. If it's not, then sad to say, it belongs in the trash. The good news is that if it's stained and bedraggled, that means you wore it out and it served its purpose.

- **Bedding** can be donated if it is in very good condition. Crib bumpers are considered a safety hazard, so they should be tossed once they've served their time or, better yet, not used at all.

- **Furniture** (especially upholstered) can be challenging to give away. Transportation of large items is a complicating factor. And beds can be seen as potential bedbug havens—in fact, even unupholstered wood furniture can be suspect. But there are many thrift stores and nonprofits that will gladly accept furniture donations, and I strongly encourage you to pursue that avenue first. Some organizations will even come and cart it away for you.

- **Toys and baby equipment** are increasingly difficult to donate. For one thing, safety regulations change and product recalls occur, which is especially an issue for strollers and car seats and some baby furniture. Anyone who remembers the lead paint scares of recent years knows that those lovely wooden trains that your child treasured might be looked at with a skeptical eye by someone else. Positively no one wants used stuffed animals (bedbugs again). Toys with small pieces (choking hazards) can also be difficult to donate. And some nonprofits will accept donations only of brand-new toys. So what to do with that old bucket of LEGOs and all those plastic dinosaurs? Maybe you have a friend or relative who would love to have them, or maybe you know of a family in need. Perhaps a local school or hospital would be interested. If not, then they, too, are destined for the trash. This is all the more reason to buy fewer toys for our children and to focus on toys that will stand the test of time (for more about this, see chapter 4). The more disposable the toy, the likelier it is to end up in a landfill.

For more advice on how best to dispose of and donate your unwanted items, go to my website: www.resourcefulconsultants.com.

Ready, Set, Go

As I said, I don't like to lecture and sermonize, I like to get to work. Now that you have the basics under your belt, it's time to follow Commandments 1 and 10 and delay no further in pursuing your dream of organizing your home. We'll begin with the space you encounter first when you walk in your front door.

2

HELLO, GOODBYE
The Entryway and Front Closet

If you took a survey of moms and asked them to describe their family's morning routines, there are a few words that I guarantee would come up over and over: Stressful. Hectic. Rushed. And if you listened in on the typical family's morning script, I bet it would go something like this (imagine these lines all shouted at once):

> *Where are my keys?*
> *My cell phone is dead!*
> *Where's my math book?*
> *I'm going to be late for the bus/train/school/meeting!*

It's no wonder mornings are so chaotic. Just look at your family's launch pad—i.e., your entryway and coat closet. What a mess, right? An archaeologist could tell a lot about your family from eyeballing the piles in your entryway—soccer pads on top of backpacks on top of sneakers; scarves on top of mail on top of keys. Meanwhile, the coat closet would require a pickax to fully excavate. It's funny that we call it a *coat* closet, because coats are the last thing most families have room for in there. Years ago I was organizing a front closet for a client and unearthed a locked trunk that was taking up a massive amount of space. My client told me that it was for "dress-up," so I suggested that we move it to the children's playroom. My client gave me a funny look and said, "It's not for the kids. It's for my husband and me." Oh.

Whatever you've got in your own coat closet or piled on your entry table, this chapter will take you through the four simple steps (purge, design, organize, maintain) to make those spaces work for you and your family. You don't need to change who you are or trade in your family members for tidier models. You just need a few commonsense systems that you can all follow—tonight, tomorrow morning, and happily ever after.

The Entryway

Every single thing that comes into our homes passes through the entryway—and often enough gets shed, plopped down, or dropped. So what's the best way to approach a space that becomes a dumping ground? Divide everything into categories and deal with them one at a time.

Mail

In a lot of entry areas, mail is the root of all evil, especially toward the end of the year, when we're bombarded with catalogs and nonprofit solicitations. The amount of paper coming into the household every day can be ridiculous. And while you're carrying groceries, your purse, maybe an umbrella and a package, what do you do with all that mail you collected? Naturally, you set it down on the nearest available surface. But this only buries things you need, such as keys, and it creates a perilous, slippery foundation for anything you put on top of it. It's a disaster waiting to happen. So let's go through the steps.

Step 1: Purge

If you already have a mound of unsorted mail in your entry area, then it's time to purge. Let's talk about how to do that.

- **Immediately recycle all catalogs, junk mail, and unwanted solicitations.** For more on reducing junk mail before it ever arrives at your door, see chapter 10.
- **Deposit magazines and newspapers where they will be read,** whether the coffee table, bedside, or perhaps directly into your purse or work bag. For more on controlling paper accumulation, see chapter 9.
- **Deliver personal mail** to the desks or bureaus of the recipients.
- **Deliver bills** and anything else that requires payment (such as organizations you wish to join or nonprofits to which you plan to donate) to your bill-paying area. For more on bill paying, see chapter 10.
- **Open your master calendar and reply to invitations** on the spot, if possible—yes or no. Invitations that require discussion with family members should go in your inbox. For more on scheduling and the master calendar, see chapter 10.

Step 2: Design

You don't need to design an infrastructure for mail in the entryway, because mail should never be left there.

Steps 3 and 4: Organize and Maintain

The key to organizing mail, and to maintaining order in the long run, is to deal with it right away. You may set your mail—briefly—on your entrance table if you have one. But once you've removed your jacket and purse or set down your bags, pick it right back up and sort it.

Shoes

When my son, Matthew, was five or six, I once found him cleaning the *bottoms* of his sneakers with Clorox wipes. (I swear: He didn't get this from me.) I reassured him that I'd be happy to clean the tops of his sneakers for him, but he could leave the bottoms alone.

The dirt we carry on our shoes is what doormats, Swiffers, and vacuums were made for. So I don't ask visitors to remove their shoes at the door. But if you're firm on going shoe-free, then you need to set some rules and put systems in place. In a lot of homes, the concept of a shoe-free household means that there's always a messy pile of shoes at the door. And there's never a good excuse for that. Let's dig in.

Step 1: Purge

Apply these guidelines for deciding what to keep, get rid of, or locate elsewhere:

- **Shoes that haven't been worn in a year** or have been outgrown should be tossed or donated.
- **Shoes that are worn regularly but are in need of repair** should be gathered together in a bag and set by the front door to be taken to the cobbler at the very next opportunity. Do not stash that bag of shoes in a closet. Act on it!
- **Foul-weather boots and shoes** should go to the front closet. For more on organizing these, see the "coat closet" section on p. 24.
- **All remaining shoes that belong to family members should go to their designated spots in the bedrooms.** And yes, this means that family members are not allowed to leave their shoes at the door—they can take them off there, but then they need to bring them to their rooms.

Step 2: Design

Guests need a place to sit down to remove their shoes, and they need a place to put their shoes once they've removed them. You might not have a lot of space in your entryway, but even a small stool will work for seating. The shoes themselves can be placed on a shoe tray on the floor or on a low shoe shelf or shoe rack. The latter two are designed to be slim enough that they can fit in a narrow hallway, and they're guaranteed to take up less space than a shoe pile.

Steps 3 and 4: Organize and Maintain

After you've purged and designed, then these steps are easy. Your guests will know what to do when they walk in, and they won't be quite so crabby while doing it, because they'll have someplace to sit. And your family members will have a clear rule to follow—take their

---

THE MYTH OF THE MUDROOM

I have space-challenged clients who salivate over the very thought of a mudroom—a separate cubby for every child, a designated storage area for shoes, a sink just for arranging cut flowers (because aren't you always arranging flowers?). But to me, unless you have a very large house, a mudroom is a waste of space and often becomes an excuse to accumulate *more* stuff and be *less* organized. An average-sized coat closet takes up far less square footage and serves the same purpose. Maybe you can't arrange flowers in there, but that's what the kitchen sink is for!

---

shoes to their bedrooms immediately upon removal. Do not pass Go; do not collect two hundred dollars.

Keys, Cell Phones, Billfolds, and Change

Although these things don't necessarily require the full purge-design-organize-maintain treatment, they can turn a tidy space into a disaster area. Here are some simple tips for keeping small items from turning into big problems.

As I mentioned in Commandment 2, routine is incredibly important to staying organized, and that is especially true when it comes to essential items such keys and phones and all that weird stuff that comes out of our husbands' pockets.

Men typically have two places where they empty their pockets—an entry table or a bureau/bedside table. **It's not your job to purge those items for your husband, but you can give him a design solution** in the form of an attractive tray where he can corral and contain them.

If that tray is in the entryway, then the table it goes on should be kept clear—nothing else should be dumped on top. A neat trick for maintaining order on an entry table is to place a vase or framed picture on it. A breakable decorative item is an automatic deterrent to anyone tempted to start a pile nearby.

Your keys and your children's keys should always be returned to the bag they're carried in every day—your purse or your child's backpack. They should never be left anywhere else. Not a hook on the wall, not a table, not a kitchen counter. They go in your bag. End of story, end of lost keys.

Similarly, **a cell phone should never be tossed on a table with a bunch of other stuff.** If you use your cell phone at home, then put it in a spot where you can find it when it's ringing, and that should always be in *the same spot*. If you don't use your cell phone at home, then there are only two places it should ever be: the charging location (which, for most families, is the kitchen counter; sometimes it's right by the computer for syncing) or back in your bag.

Purses

Though maintaining order in bags—including backpacks, which are discussed in the next section—isn't quite the same as in the rest of the home, you still need to keep the four steps in mind. You must purge regularly; you must consider the design of the bag; you must organize the contents, and you must keep purging regularly in order to maintain order.

Let's talk about **design** first, because you have control over the design of the purses and bags you buy, and that impacts everything else. I treat myself to two good purses a year, one in the winter and one in the spring. And boy, was my most recent purchase a big mistake. It's a lovely bag in a beautiful color, but it's a big bucket bag, and inevitably whatever I need at the moment is at the very bottom of that bucket. Plus, the lining is black, which is not so helpful when you're looking for your black wallet.

Purses are great fashion statements, and we all love them, but think how much energy we waste every day looking for phone, keys, wallet. Learn from my mistake and think twice the next time you consider buying a bag without interior and exterior pockets. There's nothing fashionable about constantly breaking into a cold sweat because you can't find your phone, or missing calls from your child's school or doctor—or your own boss or client—because your phone stopped ringing by the time you found it.

The best bags have a pocket on the outside that securely closes and can hold keys and whatever commuter rail, bus, or parking pass you use. Inside the main compartment of the purse, **there should be a slot for your phone and preferably a few other pockets** (for tissues and any other items you reach for often).

If, however, you have no pockets and slots because you can't give up your big bucket bag, then a good solution to that wide-open cavity is to have some **small colored pouches with zippers.** This way you know that the hot-pink one holds your makeup, and the blue one holds your tissues, Tylenol, and gum. Maybe another zippered pouch holds your keys, pen, and rail pass. The more stuff you carry around, the more you should sort and categorize items so you can find things easily.

I purposely **buy a neutral bag that goes with everything** so I don't need to switch bags all the time. This is the simplest way to stay organized and not forget essential items. If you are always switching off between bags, then keeping things in zippered pouches is all the more important, because you can move them from bag to bag. I also recommend **keeping a few duplicate items in each purse** (lip balm, tissues, even house keys). This is one time when duplication isn't such a bad idea.

No matter how many pockets your purse may have, just like your closet, it will never be organized if you stuff it with nonessentials. It's insane how much weight we drag around in our handbags, so **it's time to purge.**

1. **Take everything out of your purse.** Immediately toss all of the garbage.
2. **Look at the rest and make a pile of what you use every day** (wallet, sunglasses).
3. **Make another pile of what you really need in a pinch** (one or two bandages, eyedrops?).
4. **Put all of the above back in your purse and get rid of the rest.** It's just excess poundage.

Go through the same process with your wallet. I've hefted some women's wallets that felt like bricks, and usually, those women don't know half of what they've got in there. File essential receipts and toss the others (for more on keeping receipts, see chapter 10), and ask yourself how many of those bonus points and buy-ten-get-one-free cards you really use. By all means, get rid of the random business cards you have stuffed in there—if you need that contact information, transfer it to your address book (electronic or otherwise) and toss the card.

Remember, once you've done the initial purge of your purse and wallet and organized the contents, **regular maintenance is essential.** Daily is best for purses (that way you can discover those letters you neglected to mail and that new drugstore item you purchased and forgot to put away). A weekly purge is fine for wallets.

Children's Backpacks

In my home, my twins, Rebecca and Matthew, always leave their backpacks right in the entryway—on the floor, but out of the way of

TO MEDDLE OR NOT TO MEDDLE

You might think that a mom like me would know every item in her children's backpacks, but actually, no. I've met my match in my daughter, Rebecca, who is not only a pack rat but hates me to touch her backpack. I've learned that this battle is not worth fighting. It's my job to provide my children with bags that have adequate pockets to keep them organized. The rest is up to them. You can encourage your children to purge their backpacks each weekend, but *don't do it for them*. Either they won't appreciate it, or they'll expect you to keep doing it.

foot traffic. I don't mind, because they use their backpacks every day, so it makes practical sense to leave them out. The key, however, is that the bags always stay there, so there's never any tripping over them in the rest of the house. When Rebecca and Matthew are doing homework, they retrieve whatever they need, but the bags don't travel with them. When company comes, I usually stash the backpacks in the coat closet.

An added bonus is that **having the backpacks right by the front door can help everyone stay organized.** Once you've signed your child's permission slip, into the backpack it goes. Once your child finishes reading for the night, into the backpack the book goes. And as advised in the section on phones and keys, both of those items should always—reflexively—go right in the backpack in a designated pocket, along with your child's transportation pass, school ID, and money. If your children aren't used to keeping track of their belongings, then you'll need to remind them to do this every evening as soon as homework is done. But **in a very short time this behavior will become so ingrained that long-term maintenance is a no-brainer.**

And if you're dealing with an adolescent, a no-brainer is exactly what you need!

The Coat Closet

Enough about what sits *outside* the coat closet. Let's get inside, the event we have all been waiting for. There is probably no spot in the home that contains more random stuff. And the less storage the family has in the rest of the home, the more they expect it to contain. Remember that **no matter what you are storing, you can subject it to the Barbara Reich Eliminating-Clutter Quiz** in chapter 1. Those six simple questions are your ultimate guide to deciding what to keep and what to bid adios.

Step 1: Purge

Because the closet is such a catchall, it can be daunting to know where to begin. It's easiest to **start with the clothes.**

1. Make a pile of coats that fit, are in good repair, and are worn regularly. Unless an item is very special, if it hasn't been worn in four seasons, then you should find it a new home.

2. Make a second pile of items that you wish to donate or hand down. Check all pockets for money, gloves, etc., then wash or launder the clothing, bag it up, and send it on its way. If you have a car, put the bag right in the trunk; that way you can drop it off the next time you pass your donation recipient of choice.

3. Make a third pile of items that are unwanted and not in good repair (i.e., not worthy of donation). Check all pockets, then immediately discard that pile.

4. As you go through all the clothing in the closet, make a list of any outgrown or worn-out items that need to be replaced.

Now **let's look at the shoes.** Only foul-weather shoes should be kept here; anything else should go to the bedrooms. First make sure everything fits and is in good repair, then follow the same instructions we used for the shoe pile earlier in this chapter, getting rid of items that don't fit or are in disrepair. Make a list of any items that need to be replaced.

It's time to **take everything else out of the closet.** Follow the guidelines in chapter 1 for deciding what to keep, donate, or trash. Do not keep anything just because you think you might use it some-day. If you haven't used it in a year, then chances are you will never use it—unless it's an item expressly intended for emergencies, such as a flashlight or backup phone. Now is the time to get rid of things that are truly, inarguably junk, such as all those endless canvas tote bags you've been collecting and the random items you have stuck in-side them. Then **sort the items that you're keeping into piles—like with like.**

Step 2: Design

Now that your closet is empty and all your storage-worthy stuff is piled around you in categories, let's take a look at the inside of the closet and how you can design its infrastructure more efficiently.

Rods and Hooks

Look at where your rod is hung. Now look at the length of your coats. Evaluate the number of full-length coats—which require a lot of vertical space—versus shorter and child-sized coats, which require much less. If you currently have one long horizontal rod for all of your coats, **consider hanging a second rod** (half or two thirds as wide) from the higher rod. You can purchase very inexpensive versions from organizing stores, and they install easily, simply hooking over the higher rod. If you want a more customized height or width, you can have it constructed and installed by an expert. Either way, the beauty of hanging a second rod is that you have a few feet of rod for those full-length coats, as well as two horizontal rods that can accommodate shorter-length coats and jackets.

One typical problem in homes with young children is that their jackets end up in piles on the closet floor, because the children simply can't reach high enough to hang up their own jackets. Alternatively, Mom, you're constantly hanging up your children's jackets, which can get awfully tiresome. A better designed infrastructure is the solution. If you are able to hang a second, lower rod, then suddenly, your kids will be able to hang up their own jackets. Even if you can't, you can **install a row of hooks on the back of the closet door**—just make sure they're at the right height for your children (you can always move them up as they grow).

Coat Trees, Coat Racks, and Umbrella Stands

I usually find that a closet purge cuts down the amount of outerwear by at least a third, but many of the families I work with don't have room

---

HOW MANY UMBRELLAS DOES A CHILD NEED?

The answer to that question is zero to one, because let's face it: Who's doing most of the umbrella carrying around here? I suspect it's not your preschooler. If your children use umbrellas, then fine: They can keep one umbrella each. But I've been in homes where each child has several "play" umbrellas featuring different animated characters, and not a single one is slightly useful on a rainy, windy day. Definitely get rid of the ones that don't work in inclement weather. No five-year-old needs his own umbrella collection.

---

for all of their own coats, let alone guest coats, in the front closet. One great solution for guest coats is to **purchase a standing coat tree.** If floor space is at too much of a premium, even apartments with small, narrow entry halls can usually accommodate a **coat rack mounted on a wall** or a few hooks. I'm also a big fan of **umbrella stands.** They're attractive, they take up very little space, and they serve a purpose. There are few things that more instantly speak of an organized home then when there is a clear and tidy place to put outerwear upon entering.

Shelves

Most closets have one long shelf above the rod, and some have two. Deep, wide shelves are more difficult to organize, since items tend to get buried. If you have a single wide shelf, a quick, effective fix is to hang another shelf above it. Then you won't be forced to create teetering piles. If you don't already have room to install another shelf, you can lower your horizontal rod—even a foot or two (or whatever amount will allow you to hang those full-length coats)—so you have room to install another shelf at eye level. This is prime real estate in any closet, so it's the ideal place to have a shelf (more on what to put on that shelf when we get to step 3).

Containers and Hangers

Refer back to the Organizer's Shopping List in chapter 1. If your budget allows, purchase identical hangers. Also acquire the recommended containers. You may want to purchase a bunch prior to the next step, then return what you don't need. This is what my clients do before my first visit, so we can be sure we have enough supplies. Alternatively, you can move on to the next section and evaluate what kinds (and quantities) of containers you're most likely to need before you go shopping.

Step 3: Organize

This is the most satisfying step: putting stuff away. In a perfect world, coat closets would contain only coats, so the best way to organize this space is to reduce the variety of items you store there. If you have a basement or storage area, then by all means move rarely used items to those spaces, or opt for under-bed storage, which is a great way to maximize space. Or you might designate a cabinet in the kitchen for utility items.

Best-case scenarios aside, the reality in most homes is that you are storing items in your front closet that won't fit anywhere else. Let's look at how to store some of the most common items. For those uncommon items (such as dress-up trunks), remember that no matter what, the Ten Commandments of Organizing will always apply. Refer back to them as needed, and let's get down to organizing.

- **Foul-weather shoes.** If it's winter, then boots can stay neatly lined up on the floor of the closet. You can also add low shoe shelves or racks. However, if it's summer or you live in a warm climate, then those ski boots or off-season hiking boots don't need to be taking up floor space. Put them into labeled plastic, lidded containers for storage on an upper shelf, either here or in a bedroom closet.

- **Coats, jackets, and clothing.** Hang all those items on your nice, new matching hangers. Arrange like with like, and keep each family member's coats together, grouped by type, so that all of your jackets are next to each other. Put children's jackets on the lowest rod, and if that's not low enough, hang their jackets on hooks on the back of the door.

- **Hats, scarves, and gloves.** When my kids were younger, I had them trained. Before they hung up their jacket or coat, their hat got stuffed in a sleeve, and gloves went in pockets. This was so drilled into Matthew and Rebecca that they could do it in their sleep. If you've been able to add an eye-level shelf to your closet, then a row of bins labeled with each family member's name is a great way to organize everyone's hats, scarves, and gloves (especially for adults and older children, who might have more of these items). Alternatively, do the Squint Test (see p. 42) and create an additional storage area—an extra shelf or set of cubbyholes, for example.

- **Emergency items.** These can go into a labeled clear plastic container with a drawer, or into a labeled, lidded plastic container. In either case, the container should be placed where it can be found, preferably on the most reachable shelf. If you have room in a kitchen cabinet or utility closet to store this kit, all the better. For more on assembling and storing an emergency kit, go to chapter 7.

- **Tools.** These should go in a labeled, lidded plastic container, but they don't have to be so reachable, because truthfully, how often are you doing home repairs? Storage on an upper shelf is fine. You'll find more about tool kits in chapter 7.

- **Lightbulbs and batteries.** As noted above, small items should be stored in their own labeled clear plastic containers with drawers. Purge first so you're not storing lightbulbs for lamps you no longer have. For more ideas on storing lightbulbs and batteries, see chapter 7.

- **Sentimental items.** The closet often serves as unintentional storage for children's artwork—a bag of it comes home from school, and we stuff it into the closet until we figure out what to do with it; instead, we forget about it. Or maybe we bury our great-aunt's silver tea service that we don't use but feel too guilty to give away. Sentimental items don't really belong in this space. Go to chapter 11 for more specifics on how to cope with this kind of accumulation.

- **Dog-walking supplies.** Your dog's leash can be hung on a hook on the back of the door; waste bags and collars can be kept in a labeled bin on an eye-level shelf or hung in a mesh bag from the same hook.

- **Sporting equipment.** Your goal should be to get these items out of the closet, if at all possible. The best solution is to keep sporting equipment in the bags you or your children carry to those activities. Skates would stay in the skating bag, baseball bats and mitts, tennis rackets, etc., would all remain in their designated bags. The side benefit of this system is that you don't have to go on a full-house search for missing items when you're already late for practice. The bags themselves can be hung from a hook on the back of a bedroom or utility closet door. Off-season, those items can go in under-bed storage, or the bag can be moved to a basement or storage unit. For more on how to organize uniforms, see chapter 4.

- **Seasonal items.** Camping equipment and holiday decorations should be stored in separate clear plastic labeled boxes with lids on an upper shelf, since they don't have to be retrieved regularly. As with other rarely used items, it would be far preferable to store these things somewhere else.

- **Broken items.** Do you have a pile of random things that need to be fixed, from purses to clocks? Don't store them in the closet; leave them out in a designated area. If you haven't fixed them in two weeks, get rid of them.

- **Electronic equipment.** First, ask yourself why you are storing these items. If something is used often, it doesn't belong in a closet. If it's not used often—or ever—then you shouldn't be keeping it. There are multiple square feet of wasted space in closets around the country, all devoted to out-of-date electronic equipment. It's the modern way of life to constantly upgrade— out goes the VHS player, in comes the DVD player. Out goes the DVD player, in comes the Blue-ray player. I've been in homes where you could trace the history of the audiovisual industry in the sedimentary layers of electronic equipment they're stock-piling. Why keep the DVD player once you've got the Blu-ray player? I promise you; you will never, ever use it again. If the

DVD player is working perfectly well, then by all means donate it to someone in need. When you do so, remember to send along the accompanying cords and instruction manual.

- **Bulky items.** In many homes, the front closet is the default storage area for big things such as the vacuum cleaner, dining table inserts, water bottles, kitty litter, dog food, etc. If your closet overflows with these items, you need to prioritize. If you can store anything elsewhere, do so. As for what stays: Table inserts, when leaned against a back wall, can take up relatively little space, and clothing can be hung in front of them. The vacuum cleaner must go on the floor, there's no way around that. Empty the unwieldy bag of dog food into a large plastic container (which can be purchased at the pet store) that will be much easier to pour from. This and the kitty litter can be left on the floor, preferably tucked into a corner. Or you can install a low reinforced shelf if you've freed up some space by doing the Squint Test later in this chapter.

- **Strollers, carriers, and stroller accessories.** Assuming you have purged these items (see chapter 5) and eliminated the accessories you no longer use, your most frequently used stroller can be left outside of the closet—if there's room. Alternatively, you can fold the stroller and put it in the closet, or tuck it into a corner of the foyer (or on a closed porch or in an apartment service area, if your building allows it). Truthfully, there's no perfect solution to stroller storage unless you have endless space and/or a garage. Before very long, your children will be out of them and you can say goodbye to the strollers forever. Accessories such as rain covers and sun umbrellas can go in their own labeled bin or lidded plastic container and placed on an accessible shelf.

- **Playground toys.** These are seasonal items, and during the warmer months, you'll want them accessible. Assuming you've already purged down to what your kids really need, love, and use (for more on this concept, see chapter 4), then you can stack them neatly and place them in a bin on an accessible shelf, if one bucket is large enough to contain everything, you can hang it on a hook on the back of the closet door or tuck it into a corner of the closet (just remember, your closet doesn't have endless corners). During the colder months, these items can go into a labeled, lidded plastic container that can be stored on an upper shelf, either here or elsewhere in your home.

- **Any items not already covered in this list.** Refer back to chapter 1 for what to donate, toss, and recycle. Have you used these remaining items in less than a year? Are you keeping anything because you just can't make a decision (see Commandment 10)? Now that you've organized everything else, the remaining pile of stuff will most likely look more like junk to you. If so, you know what to do: Get rid of it.

Now that you've purged, designed, and organized the front closet, it's time to do **the Squint Test.** You can apply this test to any closet in your home. Open the doors and squint. Do you see any white space where the back wall of the closet is visible? That's wasted space. Hang clothes in size order so that you can install more storage in those areas—cubbies for shoes and accessories, or an extra shelf. Empty walls can be airy in a room, but in a closet, you want to use every inch of storage.

Step 4: Maintain

Look at your transformed entryway and coat closet. Don't you want to keep them that way? Of course you do. And you're motivated—for now. The key to keeping those fires of commitment stoked is to follow the systems you've created *on a daily basis*. This means that:

1. Everyone in the family will take their shoes to their bedrooms.
2. Everyone will return their keys and wallets to their bags or tray.
3. Mail will be sorted immediately upon delivery or arrival home.
4. Everyone will hang up their own jackets, even the littlest ones, who will now be able to reach hooks and rods.
5. Everything will be returned to its proper labeled bin or container.
6. Most important, you will never again store anything in your closet that is broken, outgrown, unwanted, obsolete, or unused.

See how easy that is?

Almost Instant Gratification

The strategies in this chapter are so easy and straightforward that they can be completed in an afternoon. Even the more complicated stuff such as putting in an extra rod can be achieved in an hour or less by a handyman. All you have to do is make a decision, make a call, and make it a priority. You'll wonder why you didn't do it sooner, because the results are just that amazing. No more frantic searches, no more avalanches (or embarrassment) as you open the closet door. All we did was eliminate a few unnecessary stressors. Life will throw you enough messes—you definitely don't need to come home to one.

3

DRESS RIGHT, SLEEP TIGHT
The Master Bedroom

There are those of us who have trouble sleeping, and those of us who have trouble getting dressed well in the morning . . . and then there are those of us who have trouble with both. Sleeping and getting dressed—are there any two elements of your day that can more powerfully affect your quality of life? To make matters more challenging, both of these enormously important tasks take place in a single room: the bedroom.

Organizing the bedroom is best broken into two projects—bringing order to the room, then streamlining the clothing storage. Once you're done with both jobs, you'll be amazed by how much calmer a space you've created. And calm is good, whether you're trying to sleep or attempting to put an outfit together.

The Room

Bedrooms can get short shrift when we're cleaning and organizing our homes, because they're private spaces. We don't hold them to the same standards as the more public areas, because when company comes, we can shut the door if need be. It's time to give your bedroom its due.

Part 1: Purge

The most common problem I see in bedrooms is that there's too much stuff. The issue is exacerbated by the fact that we tend not to think about our bedroom furniture in terms of storage capacity. We'll get to the design of the furniture later, but first let's address the various items causing disorder in your space.

Pillows

You wouldn't think that the way you make your bed could have such a big impact, but it does. Especially in a master bedroom, the bed takes up a great deal of space, and it dominates the room visually. So it stands to reason that if you pile it with decorative pillows, it's going to create a busy, disordered feeling in the room—that's what we call visual clutter. Having so many pillows also overcomplicates the process of making the bed in the morning, and forces you to dump everything on the floor when you're ready to go to bed at night. No more! The bed can have the pillows required for sleeping, plus two shams and one decorative pillow centered in front of them. Get rid of everything else.

Reading material

If you like to read in bed, then it's fine to keep a book and a few magazines on a bedside table. But when one or two items become a teetering pile, not only does it look like a mess, but it's the exact opposite of restful. Books that aren't being read currently belong on bookshelves. If unread magazines are piling up, pull out the articles you want to read and recycle the rest. For more on book and magazine storage, see chapter 9.

Lotions and toiletries

It's fine to leave a few *frequently* used items on the bedside table. They should be items you genuinely use every night, and they should be kept to a minimum. Anything else belongs in the linen closet or bathroom.

Picture frames and other decorative items

One or two pictures on your bedside or on a bureau can be nice. More than that looks like clutter, and the eye can't decide what to look at. The same holds true for vases, etc. Choose your favorite to keep where it is, and move the rest elsewhere—but before you do, subject each item to the Eliminating-Clutter Quiz from chapter 1 and decide whether they're worth keeping at all.

Once you've cleared out the visual chaos in the room, we can figure out the infrastructure that will maximize the storage potential in the room.

Step 2: Design

As I mentioned when we started the purge, a big contributor to problems in the bedroom is that we don't choose our furniture wisely. We also don't necessarily consider storage of nonclothing items. In fact, the bedroom offers more storage opportunities than you might think.

Bedside tables

Since we live in an era of multiuse furniture, there's no reason to have a bedside table that offers you nothing more than a tiny surface area. You should have a table with a minimum of one drawer and preferably more, and those drawers should be deep enough that they can hold more than a lip balm.

Bed

The open space under your bed is a fantastic storage area for plastic containers, holding anything from wrapping paper to previous-year tax returns. With a dust ruffle, no one need ever know. Some beds come with drawers built in, which is great additional storage, especially if you lack for bureaus.

Blanket chest

I don't recommend purchasing one, but if you have one already, then this is a good spot for keeping a backup sheet set plus quilts and comforters, thus freeing up space elsewhere. For more about storage of linens, see chapter 6.

Lighting

From a design perspective, I love the look of matching lamps on bedside tables, but if surface area is minimal, install wall sconces. They come in a wide range of styles and they're fantastic space savers.

Trays

There's a reason that I include trays in my list of recommended organizing tools in chapter 1. By the bedside, a small tray can corral hand lotion, reading glasses, and lip balm. On a bureau or vanity, it can hold perfume bottles and a lipstick. As we discussed in chapter 2, a tray on your spouse's side table is the best place for the keys, loose change, etc., that come out of his pockets.

A WORD ABOUT KEEPING A DESK IN THE BEDROOM

If I were a sleep doctor, I'm sure I'd tell you that the worst possible thing to have in your bedroom is a desk. But I'm not, and I know that in some households, a desk in the bedroom is non-negotiable. If that's you, then go to chapter 10 for advice on organizing your home office. And definitely choose a desk with drawers so you can make sure those bills and papers are out of sight—and out of mind—when it's time to sleep.

Ereaders and tablets

These are the perfect solution to that teetering pile of reading material by your bedside.

Steps 3 and 4: Organize and Maintain

Once you've reduced the number of things in your room and you have furniture that better serves your needs, organizing and maintaining the space is simple. There's a place for everything, including ample interior storage so that not everything has to be on display. Now your job is to 1) keep a firm handle on the stuff you bring into the room, and 2) return everything to its appointed spot. When your reading material starts stacking up, purge it back down to one or two items. If your bedside table starts looking like the inside of your medicine cabinet, return those items where they belong. And if you're out shopping and you see a lovely pillow that would look fantastic on your bed, you're allowed to buy it only if you're prepared to get rid of the one you already have.

That's not so horrible, is it? A serene space is your very desirable reward for a little bit of effort on a daily basis.

Clothing Storage

A large percentage of my clients would identify their clothes closets as their personal hot spots of disorder. We might avert our eyes when passing the messy utility closet, but on a daily basis, we can't avoid the frustration of finding something to wear to the various events we're required to attend—business meetings, school events, weddings, funerals.

Moms have it harder than any other member of the family in this regard. Number one, it's just a fact that it's more complicated to dress well as a woman than a man. Far more creativity is expected of us, there's way more that can go wrong, and when we do miss the mark, we're scrutinized more harshly. Number two, women's dress codes are more variable—or at least that's what magazines would have us believe. Figuring out what to wear to brunch versus the park versus dinner with friends versus casual Friday can seem like advanced math. It's no wonder Hollywood actresses hire professionals to help them pick what dress to wear.

Some moms I know give up altogether. If they're not going to an office, then they're in yoga pants 24/7. Others never give up trying, but they torture themselves in the process, spending too much money and cramming their closets with stuff in an endless, seemingly fruitless search for the magic combination of clothes that will make them smile when they look in the mirror.

It's logical but somehow hard to believe that the secret to having something to wear in the morning is not to buy *more* clothing, it's to buy less—and store less. You just have to choose the right items so that your smaller, more edited collection of clothing serves you better (more on this when we get to step 3). So let's open up those closet doors and see what you've got in there.

SEEKING A SECOND OPINION

If you want to invite a friend to help you purge and evaluate your wardrobe, that's fine, but be sure your friend is honest and can be trusted to think of your style, not her own. Though your friend may think that frilly blouse is adorable on you, if it gives you hives, then trust your instincts. It could be a perfectly lovely blouse, but if your style leans more toward tailored than girlie, those hives are telling you something. Chances are, the styles that make you feel best and most comfortable are also the ones that look best on you.

Step 1: Purge

These are the top two reasons that most of us have too much clothing:

1. We're hoping to be (or afraid to be) a different size.
2. We're really not sure what looks good on us, or works best for our lifestyle, so we continue buying and keeping things that we don't feel comfortable wearing.

Sometimes, before we can purge our clothes, we have to grapple with our emotions. When you're faced with an overstuffed closet, it's important not to get bogged down. The issue isn't what size you were a year or more ago, or what size you might be six months from now. The questions are: What size are you right now? What looks good on you today? What suits the life you lead?

For many women, a big complicating factor is **maternity clothes,** as well as those in-between sizes that you wear either before you're in maternity clothes or in the months after you have the baby. If you are planning to have more children, you will want to store those items in labeled clear plastic containers, preferably by size and season. Once you're done having babies, sort those items and donate what is in good condition, then get rid of the rest.

Most of us don't feel burdened by keeping clothes that are too big for our current bodies—it's the clothes that are too small that we hang on to tooth and nail. Maybe you're in the middle of a weight-loss program or planning to start one, and you're sure those clothes will eventually fit again. And maybe you're right. But if you do lose weight, wouldn't it be better to buy yourself some new, flattering items rather than wear clothing that's already seasons—even years—out of style? **If you've been holding too-small clothing in reserve for over a year, it's time to say goodbye.**

Some of my clients feel guilty about getting rid of perfectly good clothing, especially if it was never worn. Maybe someone you love gave it to you and it doesn't suit you. Or maybe you bought the item for yourself only to realize too late that it doesn't go with your life or your wardrobe. And there it hangs, tags still on, mocking you every time you open the closet door. Don't let this happen! **You are in control of your clothing, not vice versa.**

Let's put all those emotions aside and get realistic.

1. **Pull out everything in your closet and drawers.** If you haven't worn a piece in a while and aren't sure whether to keep it, try it on and assess whether it fits and flatters.

2. **Make one pile of all the clothing that is too small or too large or just doesn't look good on you or suit your style.** If you haven't worn an item in a year, then there is a reason for that. Be brutally honest with yourself, and remember Commandment 8: Ignore sunk costs. It doesn't matter how much

you paid for it if it doesn't flatter you. These items should go in a bag for donation.

3. **Make another pile of items that are pilled, stained, or torn** beyond repair. Check pockets first, then immediately trash.

4. **Examine your T-shirts and underpinnings.** Toss anything past its prime. And if you've been waiting a month for that other sock to show up to make a pair, it's time to give up on it.

5. **Group like with like and look for duplicates.** Sort the keepers into categories: cardigans, T-shirts (long-sleeved and short), jeans, etc. Invariably, this is educational. We all have our items that we keep buying over and over—for me, it's black sweaters. But no one needs more than three sweaters or pants of the same color that serve the same purpose. Most people have way too many basics, T-shirts and socks especially. If you have a washer and dryer and do your laundry at least once a week, you don't need much more than a week's worth of underpinnings and certainly not more than two weeks' worth. Keep the best and toss the rest.

6. **Look at your shoes.** How many sneakers do you need and wear? How many black boots? Are any in need of repair or retirement? Don't stash them away again; either toss them or put them in a bag by the front door, then take them to the cobbler the next time you leave.

7. **Purge your scarves, purses, belts, and jewelry in the same way.** Some of those items take up very little space, but if you don't wear them or they're no longer your style, why not give

them away (or consider reselling if the item has value). This way, when you reach for a scarf or a necklace, you're choosing from your absolute favorites and vastly increasing the chances that you'll choose the one that *most* flatters you.

8. **While you're making your piles, keep a shopping list** of things you might need to replace or add to your wardrobe in order to fill out outfits. You'll need this list when we get to step 3.

If you're having difficulty making decisions about what items to keep or eliminate, refer back to the Eliminating-Clutter Quiz in chapter 1. I'll give you a little extra help with the toughest question, which is, never fail, number 3 (Will I ever use it/wear it?). This is the one my clients constantly trip over. I call it the *Green Eggs and Ham* Effect.

I BOUGHT IT ON SALE, SO I'M SAVING MONEY, RIGHT?

How familiar does this sound: You're shopping at a discount store or the sale rack of your favorite department store. You come across a jacket from the kind of designer featured in *Vogue* magazine. It doesn't fit you well, but you think maybe you can alter it. Or maybe it's a blouse in a color, print, or cut that isn't your style. Or a purse in acid green. It's 80 percent off and so beautifully made . . . what to do? I'll tell you what to do: Don't buy it! A bargain is a bargain only if you would have bought it at full price (had you the budget). Here's the rule of thumb to follow when buying on sale: If you genuinely love it and have someplace to wear it *and* it fills a gap in your wardrobe, buy it. If you love it but have nowhere to wear it and you're not the adventurous type, put it back. And if you don't love it and/or it doesn't fit, *put it back.*

Clients' scenarios for when they *could* wear it will come fast and furious in a last-ditch attempt to justify keeping an item: *Will I wear it on a boat? Will I wear it on a float?* I'll hold up a sequined spaghetti-strap dress that has never been worn (or was last worn on New Year's Eve 1996), and a perfectly sane woman who hates the water and has never taken a cruise will try to convince me that she might wear it if she ever does. Into the donate pile it goes.

Steps 2 and 3: Design and Organize

Once you've purged, it can be quite satisfying to put away all your clothing and accessories. That's especially the case if your purging has yielded more space in your closet and drawers, and suddenly, you don't have to squash and stuff. There are two kinds of clothing storage—hanging and folding—and several ways of storing shoes and accessories. Let's take a look at each.

Folding

There are certain items that are just better folded—underpinnings, T-shirts, sweaters, and shorts. If you have a lot of folding storage, jeans can go in this category as well, which will free up some room in your closet. Here are some more tips for planning out your folding storage in the most efficient way possible:

- **Beware of bureaus with drawers that are too deep.** The deeper you have to stack items in a drawer, the harder it is to find and retrieve things on the bottom.

- **Assign three or four drawers for each adult** to store lingerie, socks, sleep clothes, and exercise clothes. If your bureau isn't large enough, consider selling the one you have and purchasing something larger.

- **Take advantage of drawer organizers.** They're not absolutely necessary if you're on a budget, but if your drawers are wide, these can help keep your clothing clearly organized. You can find bra dividers, sock dividers, and on and on. If you do purchase them, make sure they all match in style.

- **Fold socks and buy in multiples.** You read me right: *Fold* your socks. Rolled-up socks make drawers a mess, and rolling wears out the elastic. As for buying in multiples, how much time do you spend matching your family's socks when you're folding the laundry? What a headache. There is one incredibly easy solution: Buy each family member only one kind of dress sock and one kind of athletic sock. If your family complains that this is too restrictive, tell them to fold their own darn socks.

- **There are two ways to fold T-shirts,** depending on how you're storing them. On shelves, they can be stacked (folded edge facing out) so you can easily see what you've got. In drawers, I like to fold them filing cabinet–style: Fold your T-shirt as you normally would, then fold it in half again and "file" it in your drawer, folded edge facing up.

- **Store knit tops and sweaters on shelves.** If you don't have shelves, you can purchase a freestanding wardrobe, or you can add shelving to an existing closet if you are willing to give up some rod width. Alternatively, you can purchase canvas hanging shelves to suspend right from your closet rod. Your jeans can go on these as well; they make things so much more visible.

Hanging

Whether you and your spouse share a closet or you have your own, you can design your portion to suit your needs. Here's how:

- **Purchase matching hangers for everything in the closet,** when your budget allows. Ideally, these will match the type used in all the other closets in the house, and you can move hangers around as needed.

- **Consider lowering your top rod,** as we did in chapter 2— thereby allowing you to add an extra shelf at eye level, perfect for storing jeans and sweaters.

- **Calculate how much full-length hanging space you need for your clothing.** You can then hang a second, lower rod from the top rod that is half the length or less. This simple adjustment effectively doubles the amount of space you have to hang shorter items such as blouses and jackets. As noted in chapter 2, double hanging rods can be purchased cheaply from specialty organizing stores.

- **Arrange like with like,** and within each category of clothing, sort by color from light to dark. Each morning you'll know exactly where to go for those pants, that top, and the cardigan or jacket that you'll top it off with.

- **Remember the Squint Test** in chapter 2? Now do the same in your clothes closet. Are there any white spaces that could be filled with additional shelving? Can you move existing shelves closer together? Shelves at eye level that are meant for stacked clothing don't need to be over twelve inches apart. Maximize open areas by adding hooks for scarves or cubbies for purses.

- **Make room for out-of-season clothing.** I don't store off-season clothing; I keep it all in one closet. This is practical because so much clothing is three-season. It also serves to keep me disciplined in terms of quantity. If your closet is too small to contain all your clothing, then it's fine to store off-season items in labeled under-bed containers or in labeled plastic containers on high shelves.

Shoes

Often shoe storage isn't built in to the design of the closet, so shoes are piled up on the floor. **The two best options for shoes are stackable shelves and/or stackable shoe cubbies.** If you have extra space on your rod, you can purchase hanging shoe cubbies. For shoes with a lower profile (sandals, flats, dress heels, and some sneakers), cubbies are best because shoes can be spooned together, taking up less space. If boots or shoes are too large to fit in standard shoe cubbies, stackable shoe shelves or racks can work really well. One neat trick is to **face the two halves of a pair upright and in opposite directions so they hug each other's curves.** This can save several inches of storage when multiplied over several pairs of shoes.

Accessories

Accessories vary greatly in shape and size, so let's consider what works best for each.

- **Jewelry.** Depending on how much jewelry you have, a standard **jewelry box** may not be enough for you. Some necklaces and bracelets can be safely hung on **jewelry trees,** which you'll find in many stores and in all shapes and styles. You can also hang an attractively wood-framed **peg board** with a velvet or textile background. These look quite nice on a wall over a bureau or next to the mirror where you do your hair or makeup, if that's in the bedroom. Often these peg boards have glass doors that close, keeping jewelry safe from dust and dirt, and the pegs can accommodate necklaces as well as a large earring collection. If you prefer concealed storage, especially for pricier items and things that might tarnish, then **jewelry trays** can be stacked inside bureau drawers and can also be labeled.

- **Scarves.** These can be stacked on a shelf or hung—you can purchase special hangers—and organized by type and weight.

- **Belts.** Men's belts tend to be uniform in size and can be rolled and stored in drawers—you can buy dividers for this purpose— or hung, either on a special hanger or on an organizer mounted on the back of the closet door. Women's belts, which range in width and may have elaborate buckles, tend to be better off hung on a belt hanger or from a rack mounted on the back of a closet door.

- **Ties.** These can be rolled and stored in a drawer, or hung on a hanger designed for ties, depending on where you have more storage space.

No matter what type of accessory you're storing, remember that the more visible and accessible it is, the more likely you are to wear it.

Step 4: Maintain

While maintaining order in a space is easy once you've done the first three steps, things get a little more challenging when it comes to clothing and accessories. After all, we don't decorate our bodies once and leave them that way until we're ready to redecorate. We have to get dressed every day, and for vastly different occasions, and we change the mix of our wardrobes fairly often. So how can we stay on top of things in the long term and in such a way that our daily lives are made easier?

As I noted at the start of this chapter, one of the reasons that moms have such a hard time with their wardrobes is that we're led to believe that it's complicated to put together appropriate outfits for the myriad responsibilities in our lives. But it doesn't have to be. Look around you. The women you'd call the most stylish are the ones who have their own look, and that look tends not to vary too much. Those women aren't trying to reinvent the wheel every day, so it doesn't take a whole lot of items to keep them looking good day in and day out. All they need are a handful of tried and true combinations and maybe a scarf or necklace or two.

Maintaining control of your clothing storage now and in the future is all about finding your own style. **When you know what works for you and looks good on you, there's no need for the endless searching—and purchasing—that results in an overstuffed closet.** Since I spend most of my time visiting clients, I hit upon a "uniform" a few years ago that works for me but still looks put together in the urban environment where I live. It's nothing fancier or more complicated than dark jeans, boots, a thin sweater or blouse, and a jacket. In the summer my uniform changes to white jeans, a stylish T-shirt or blouse, and wedges. Getting dressed in the morning is an absolute cinch.

Outfits like these might not be brain surgery to the naturally fashionable, but they took me a while to figure out. When I first left the corporate world, I held on to all my old suits until I realized that I wasn't wearing them anymore. At this point in my life, I've learned that I need only a tightly edited selection of *current* outfits that will take me from a corporate environment to a *Today* show appearance. That's what I've got. And when I wear out those outfits or they're no longer in style, I'll start shopping for new items to rotate in.

Your work, dress, and casual needs might be different from mine, but the central point is the same. **Once you settle on the ingredients of the perfect uniform for each aspect of your life, then getting dressed will be a breeze,** and you'll always know that you're wearing clothing that suits you and your lifestyle.

For a little help with finding a uniform that works, I asked an expert to give me a cheat sheet of items that every woman should consider tried and true. Shari Schmeltzer has been a personal shopper at Bergdorf Goodman for the past fourteen years. Not only is she enviably stylish herself, and endlessly patient in teaching others, she's also admirably practical. She knows that no matter how expensive or stylish an item is, if it's not wearable and versatile, then there's no point in having it. Shari is a big fan of having fewer items in your closet and having them all work for you in a variety of ways. Here is her list of what every woman should ideally have. Your individual life and work might require some alterations (and you might prefer red pumps to leopard-print), but consider this list an excellent starting point:

- ☐ Two pairs of jeans, one skinny or straight, and one flared or boot-cut
- ☐ Basic black cardigan
- ☐ Black dress that's super-flattering and can be dressed up or down
- ☐ Black dress pants
- ☐ Crisp white button-down
- ☐ Layering T-shirts in basic colors
- ☐ Silk patterned or colored blouse
- ☐ Black patent heel
- ☐ Leopard-print heel
- ☐ Comfortable ballet flat
- ☐ Fitted leather jacket (can be worn over a dress, with dress pants, or with jeans)
- ☐ Classic trench coat

☐ Handbag for day
☐ Evening clutch
☐ Statement necklace

Now comes the fun part. Compare Shari's list to your wardrobe. Are you missing any items that could help pull together some outfits? Add them to the list you made when you were purging, and put it on your smartphone. Consider this your **shopping list.** No, you probably can't—and shouldn't—acquire everything at once. But the next time you're flipping through a sale rack, or you happen to stop into your favorite clothing store, consider the list your conscience, and don't ignore it or veer from it. A little bit of discipline is the way to maintain a streamlined wardrobe.

DIY DIGITAL LOOK BOOK

There are some impressively stylish women out there who devote whole blogs to documenting their outfits each day. These women are far more creative with their clothing than I will ever be, but even the stylistically challenged among us can take a lesson from them. We tend to focus a lot of our emotional energy on the days when we don't look our best. Instead, lavish more attention on those days when everything seems to work—when you get several unexpected compliments, or you catch a look of yourself in a store window and think, *Huh, I look pretty good today!* The next time that happens, snap a picture of yourself on your smartphone. That way you won't forget the secret formula that yielded such a great look. Over time, the pictures might help you identify the distinctive look or style that really suits you. Next thing you know, you'll be posting them on Facebook . . . or not. But I bet those compliments will start to become a more daily occurrence. At a minimum, having a handful of reliable outfits in mind will make getting dressed in the morning faster and easier.

The Keys to Happiness

Think about the people you see in your everyday life who seem to have it all figured out. Now picture how they look. Are they haggard and unkempt? Probably not. Feeling well rested and pulled together might not be the *only* keys to happiness, but they sure do communicate it to the world. Moms carry a world of responsibility on their shoulders, but a good night's sleep and a few snappy outfits can at least make that load *look* a lot lighter. And when you catch a look at yourself in the mirror and you like what you see, that load might just *feel* a bit lighter, too.

4

A WALK ON THE WILD SIDE
Children's Bedrooms
and Play Areas

We all have different ways of wanting to live our lives, and we try not to judge the way our neighbors live theirs (I did say *try*, didn't I?). But I dare you to walk into someone else's home and not make some assumptions about that household based on how the children's toys are arranged and how many toys they have. Who among us receives the most judgment from the larger world? Moms, of course.

As I've noted, some families have more space than others. Some have a family room as well as a living room. Some children share rooms and some have their own. But if I had to divide families with children into two different categories, they would be: 1) those who separate children's stuff into designated areas, and 2) those who don't mind having children's things in the common living areas. From my point of view, there's nothing wrong with either approach, as long as it works for your space.

It's up to you to figure out the kind of home you want. Do you want to have one living space in the house that is totally toy-free? We can accomplish that. Alternatively, do you want your living spaces to be multiuse? We can accomplish that, too, and we can do it in such a way that your living room doesn't start to look like Toys "R" Us after a flood.

Before we get to your children's play areas, let's tackle two other regions that can cause both mess and frustration: 1) children's clothing storage, and 2) their work spaces. Once you've completed the whole process, I won't claim that clothing will never again end up on the floor, or that homework will never again end in tears, but I promise there will be a lot fewer causes for argument.

Clothing Storage

If you've already gone through the steps of organizing your clothing storage in chapter 3, then you have a good sense of how to approach the task of organizing children's clothing. The steps here are essentially the same, with a few tweaks.

Step 1: Purge

Empty the drawers, closet, and/or wardrobe. Now:

1. Sort all the items into piles by category as well as by size if you have items that your child hasn't grown into.
2. All items that have been outgrown but are in good enough condition to be donated or handed down should go into a

separate pile (for more on the subject of hand-me-downs, see chapter 5).

3. Into another pile, put anything that is outgrown and stained or torn beyond wearability. Now toss.

4. Look at the piles of clothing that are in good condition and fit your child. Are there any items that your child hates and refuses to wear? Put those in a separate pile. You can keep clothing that is meant strictly for special occasions; while your son may hate wearing a suit, sometimes he has to. But if it's an everyday item and it's languishing unworn, don't keep it; donate it. And pay attention to your child's dislikes—i.e., your son refuses to wear anything that buttons at the collar, or your daughter hates anything stiff—and avoid purchasing similar items in the future.

5. Do a count of what remains, and look for holes in your child's wardrobe. Make a shopping list, and *stick to it.*

Step 2: Design

Closets are rarely made to accommodate children's small clothing and statures. This creates two problems: 1) a ton of vertical space is wasted when there's just one high rod; and 2) children can't reach high enough to put away their own clothing, so Mom gets stuck doing all the work. As I addressed in chapter 2, there's an easy remedy for both of these problems: **Install low hooks on the back of closet doors, and double-hang the rods** in the closet so you can store many more small items. Also, **do the Squint Test** (see chapter 2) and find any open areas for additional storage—cubbies for shoes, shelves for folded items or to hold labeled bins for uniforms or non-clothing items.

And, of course, **buy only one type of hanger.**

Step 3: Organize

Generally speaking, **very small clothing is better hung;** it gets too bulky when folded, and a deep drawer can turn into a black hole for smaller-sized items.

Older kids with larger clothing find **free-standing wardrobes or a vertical row of shelves** in a closet really user-friendly—items can be categorized and stacked in such a way that everything is clearly visible and easily accessible, and shelves can be labeled.

If you've double-hung the rods in your child's closet, **place the most frequently used, in-season items where they're most reachable.** Out-of-season clothing and dressier items can go on the upper rod.

This is less of an issue for older kids, but storing multiple sizes of clothing for babies and toddlers can get tricky. We've all groaned with frustration on discovering the adorable onesie that was too big when we received it as a gift and two sizes too small when we next unearthed it. The best way to address this problem is to **separate the clothing not just by type but by size.** If the items are folded on a shelf or in a drawer, you can label each stack. If the items are in the closet, you can hang things in size order—smallest to largest—after dividing them into categories.

A special word about **organizing sports uniforms:** This is a big issue, especially for families with multiple children who might participate in more than one sport or activity. As noted in chapter 2, sporting equipment should be stored in whatever bag your child carries to the activity. All the components of the uniform, however, should be kept in a single location, whether that spot is a labeled bin on a closet shelf or its own designated drawer. This way, your child isn't left to dig in the sock drawer for the soccer socks and the shirt drawer for the baseball jersey. Children know that **the entire uniform can be found in**

one place. This saves a huge amount of stress when everyone is rushing to make it to practice or a game on time.

Step 4: Maintain

Your long-term goal should be providing your children with the routines and infrastructure that allows them to find what they need, to dress themselves, and to put things away where they belong. To that end, the simpler and clearer you make systems for your children—with the right shelving and labels for where categories of clothing are supposed to go—the better. You'll be amazed how quickly your children will learn to cooperate. Even the most organizationally lax have to admit that life is a whole lot easier when they can find their sweatpants on gym day.

Very young children are expected to **hang their own jackets** when they go to school, and you should expect the same thing from them at home. Now that your children have hooks and rods they can reach, the task is made much easier. Another important maintenance routine to teach children is to **wear their clothing in the order in which it was washed.** Freshly laundered T-shirts should be placed on the bottom of the T-shirt pile so that the same two aren't worn over and over again.

Children can be helpful in other ways. It should be reflexively drilled into them that **all uniforms go directly into the wash when they're dirty,** and they get returned to their designated storage spot when they're clean. I have a rule in my house: **If an item of clothing or a pair of shoes is too small, it doesn't get put back in the drawer or closet.** It's given right to me, and then I determine whether it should be tossed or given away.

There is one area of maintenance that is really the parents' responsibility: clothing purchases. Babies zip through sizes so quickly that you're always buying new clothing, but you should shake yourself out of that mentality once your children reach school age. **Apply the same purposeful attitude toward buying for your children that you have developed for yourself.** Yes, there will be the sudden growth spurts that require you to replenish what's been outgrown, but you shouldn't be buying clothing for your children year-round. Beyond replacing what doesn't fit and what's worn out, there are three times of the year to shop for clothing:

1. **August.** Back to school, which is also the right time to evaluate outerwear from the previous winter and determine if your child needs a new coat.
2. **December/January.** When gifts might be given and it could be time to replace items outgrown in the fall, or to prepare for a vacation to a different climate.
3. **May/June.** Getting ready for summer.

Finally, remember that children's clothing preferences can turn on a dime. When my daughter, Rebecca, was five, she wore nothing but dresses. After I bought her a bunch, she decided she was done with dresses and would wear only pants. Lesson learned. If you restrict yourself to buying *what* your children need, *when* they need it, you'll have a lot less purging and organizing to do. And you'll have taught yourself and your children a valuable lesson about restraint.

Work Spaces

Art projects and homework can occur anywhere in the home, and often the least likely place for these activities is the child's bedroom. Let's look at each work space separately.

Art Projects

I've been in many homes where the moms in particular feel like it's their duty to provide every conceivable art supply for their children. We all want to encourage our children's creativity, but you don't need to turn your home into an art room; that's what preschool and art classes are for.

Step 1: Purge

To purge well, you have to give yourself permission to narrow down the kinds of art projects you allow in your home. I promise you, this is perfectly reasonable, and no one will report you to Children's Services. For the same reason you don't let your children play baseball in the living room, you don't have to give them art materials that are guaranteed to make a mess. Here's what to do:

- Get rid of anything that would be a disaster if it were dropped or the cap popped open. I'm talking about buckets of paint and those precarious tubes of glitter—the bane of my existence. If you don't have these things, you won't have to clean them up; it's as simple as that.

- If you already have an easel, if you have adequate space for it, and if your kids use it *regularly,* then you are allowed to keep it. Otherwise, donate it to someone else. Easels take up a lot of room, and in my experience, children are just as happy drawing on a table or even the floor.

- Sort through all Magic Markers, colored pencils, and crayons, and toss any that are dry, too worn down to be usable, or broken.

- Sort through Model Magic, Play-Doh, and other modeling media, and toss any that are dry or unusable.

- Pull out all the coloring, activity, sticker, and invisible-ink books and recycle those that are used up or no longer used at all. Also consider tearing out and recycling the used pages in the coloring books that you plan to keep, since children are much more likely to use books when they don't have to search for clean pages. A word to the wise: Invisible ink isn't invisible on upholstered furniture!

- Sort through all drawing pads and pull out the artwork you wish to keep, recycling the rest of the used paper.

- As you purge, make a list of anything that needs to be replaced or replenished.

Steps 2 and 3: Design and Organize

Now that you've purged everything, what is the best location for the storage you plan to design? Ideally, you should follow Commandment 6 and **store things where you use them.** If the art projects are done at the kitchen table, designate a cabinet in that room for supplies. If you have a playroom, then the obvious choice is to establish a few shelves of storage there. If you have a very young child who needs supervision during art projects, the least desirable place to store these things is in the child's bedroom, since you might not always be there to oversee. However, you can designate a few shelves in an older child's bedroom or closet.

Here's a list of the art supplies that you might like to have on hand and how to store and organize them:

- **Colored pencils, Magic Markers, and crayons.** Think quality over quantity and buy sets that come in sturdy, user-friendly packaging. Then you can keep them in labeled clear plastic drawers. When the child is ready to use something, she can pull out the whole drawer, leaving behind the case that holds it.

- **Modeling media.** These can be stored in a labeled plastic drawer or a labeled, lidded plastic container, or in a labeled bin if you are storing it on a shelf and the items are used often.

- **Coloring books and activity books.** Sort these by type and keep them in paper trays or baskets on a shelf, or in magazine organizers. Just remember Commandment 9 and make sure the organizers all match.

- **Drawing pads and paper.** I like using stacking trays for plain, colored, and lined paper. Smaller drawing pads can be stored here as well. And while small children love large pads, they can be a pain to store. Buy just one at a time, and store it against a wall behind your child's bedroom door.

Step 4: Maintain

Once you've designed the storage, it shouldn't be difficult for you and your children to keep things organized in the long term. Your job is to replenish supplies as needed. There are only two rules to instill in your children:

1. Don't put back anything that's dry, broken, or unusable. Throw it away.
2. When you're done with something, put it away.

Now all you have to figure out is what on earth to do with all the artwork your children create. For more on that sticky wicket, go to chapter 11.

Homework

If you ask any mom what she most frequently fights about with her school-aged children, the word "homework" comes up over and over. There are some kids who don't murderously hate it. But even the best students will throw a fit about it now and then, and often it's Mom who absorbs the anxiety and feels responsible.

No amount of organization is going to make your children whistle while they work, but there are things you can do to make the pill go down easier—and make your own life calmer in the process.

We can skip Step 1, because that's not an issue here. But steps 2 and 3 can have a big impact.

Step 2: Design

Your children need a clear place to do their homework. Many parents focus too much on getting their children to work at their desks, and lots of children rebel. This is totally understandable to me, because most child-sized desks don't provide adequate surface area. Also, a child who isn't that keen on doing homework in the first place doesn't want to feel locked away in his or her room. **It's perfectly fine if your children want to do the homework at the dining room or kitchen table.**

The important thing is that **homework is done at a set place every day, and at a set time**—preferably as soon as children get home (or after they've had a snack and a few minutes to unwind). Routine is one of the best ways I know of to curb arguments; it's only when things are unclear and inconsistent that there's anything to negotiate or fight about.

Step 3: Organize

Another stress preventer is to **make sure your children have the supplies they need and know where to find them.**

- ☐ **Loose-leaf and printer paper.** These can be stored in stacking trays.
- ☐ **Highlighters, permanent markers, pens, and pencils.** These can be stored in decorative canisters, or in a desk drawer with dividers, or in small stacking drawers, which can be found in office supply and home organization stores.
- ☐ **A few sheets of poster board.** In truth, I hate the whole concept of poster board. It's large, bulky, difficult to store, and can't we all use PowerPoint? I would ban poster board if I could, but I also know that many a Sunday-night homework crisis could be averted if we all kept a few of these rolled up and tucked in a closet or on top of a bookcase.

Step 4: Maintain

A calmer and more serene and orderly approach to homework in the long term isn't an impossible goal. It just takes a little follow-up.

- As you've done with art supplies, get your children in the habit of tossing broken or inkless pens and stubby, eraserless pencils. That way anything that your children pick up is usable, thus avoiding those recurrent shrieks of "HOW COME NONE OF THESE PENS EVER WORK?"

- If your older children have been given a homework planner by their school, encourage them to use it and refer to it often, both before and after homework, to be certain they haven't forgotten anything.

- Most important, make sure you're creating an environment in which your child can focus, by providing the necessary tools as well as a quiet, clutter-free space.

Play Spaces

For families with young children, this is the biggie, right? I've been overwhelmed by the quantity of toys I've seen in homes large and small. Moms will simultaneously complain about the accumulation and insist that they can't possibly get rid of anything for fear their children will be grief-stricken. You can't have it both ways. My constant refrain is: **You can have a home or you can have a toy museum.**

The fact is, the more stuff children have, the less they appreciate what they do have, and the less easily they can enjoy the few toys that they really love. So if the goal is to make our children happy—and that's what we're all thinking when we get our children new toys—we're not accomplishing it by giving them more, more, more. So let's go through the steps. I promise you'll be glad you did.

Step 1: Purge

How do you purge your children's toys without upsetting them? Honestly, it's a lot easier than you think, and I'll give you a classic example—one of my favorite stories from all my years of professional organizing.

My client Hilary is an accumulator. She can't stop buying, whether it's pictures from Shutterfly, lice shampoo, clothes, or toys. I have threatened more than once to put a lock on her computer so she can't buy anything online. In addition to her own purchasing habits, she has extremely generous in-laws. So generous, that they bought her children not just one but two ginormous stuffed gorillas. They're almost life-size, and they cost thousands of dollars.

When organizing the playroom, I asked Hilary if she was ready to part with the gorillas. Although her children didn't play with them, she said they "liked them." Well, of course they liked them. By definition, a toy is something a child likes. After much discussion, Hilary finally said that she thought she could get rid of one gorilla without her children being too upset. We put the gorilla outside on the curb in the hopes that someone would come along and make a home for it. Then Hilary got into the spirit of paring down and decided to put the other gorilla outside, too.

Fast-forward a few hours to when Hilary picked up her four-year-old daughter, Lily, from school. As they were walking home, they saw a homeless man outside with the two gorillas and a sign that said $20 OR BEST OFFER. Lily noticed the man and said, "Mommy, those are just like our gorillas." Hilary was sweating and praying that no one would buy the gorillas before she had time to go back and get them. They went home, and her daughter asked where *their* gorillas were. Then the phone rang, the baby woke up, the babysitter left, the TV went on, and both Lily and Hilary forgot all about the gorillas. P.S., Lily never asked about them again.

Though I find this story hilarious and edifying, I'm not suggesting that you toss out your children's toys without asking them first. I would hate to see you forced to do the parental equivalent of the "walk of shame"—i.e., trying to retrieve a toy from the trash on the side of the street. It is proof, though, that even something as massive and unmissable as a stuffed gorilla isn't nearly as missed as you think it will be.

With that in mind, let's **look at your pile of toys and purge.** We're going to number the list, because going in this order makes things more manageable.

1. **Start making piles by category** (such as shape sorters; dolls and accessories; action figures, etc.). When you find random small pieces, you'll gradually be able to match them with the toys to which they belong.

2. **Make a pile of items that are obviously junk** and should be trashed. What's junk? All games and toys with so many missing pieces that they're not usable or fun anymore, broken toys, and just about anything that came in a goodie bag or was won at a carnival.

3. **Make a pile of duplicate toys and games** to give away or to keep at a grandparent's house—this includes the five different versions of Monopoly.

4. **Do your children—and yourself—a favor and get rid of all so-called educational toys.** I'm not talking about toys that are developmentally wonderful for your children, such as puzzles and shape sorters and building toys. I'm talking about flash cards and "activity books" and things that positively scream EDUCATIONAL in a way that sends your child running in horror. These are also known as "toys that exist to make you feel guilty." Trust that if it doesn't look fun to you, it will not look fun to your child.

5. **Sort the stuffed animals** and keep only those that your child genuinely cares about. Anything else is just collecting dust,

and your child will not miss them (see aforementioned life-size gorilla).

6. **Now evaluate the large toys that live on the floor**—train tables, play kitchens, play castles, etc. Eliminate anything that isn't played with regularly, i.e., on a daily basis. Otherwise, if it's as big as a piece of furniture, it's not justifying the space it occupies. Definitely eliminate duplicates. No family needs more than one play kitchen.

7. **Books should get the same treatment as toys.** Sort them into piles according to keep, donate, and toss (if they're ripped or otherwise not worthy of donation). If you find duplicates, which is inevitable, consider keeping a few backups in the family car or at grandparents' homes.

8. **Once you've purged everything else** . . . If you are left with a mound of hundreds of unsorted items—tiny LEGO pieces, unmatched doll socks, an ear from Mr. Potato Head, and a host of unidentifiable plastic shapes—ask yourself if it's worth your time to go through it all. If not, then toss it. All of it. I swear: You and your children won't miss a thing.

Once you've purged, if you still feel that you have way more stuff than you have room, it's time to get ruthless. Consider eliminating:

✂ all the toys that your children like but don't love.
✂ the toys that they've basically outgrown but play with now and then.
✂ the toys that they play with only when they see them in the donate pile.

TURN DECLUTTERING INTO A GIVING EXPERIENCE

Getting rid of toys doesn't have to be a downer for your children (or for you). You can turn the process of cleaning your child's room into an opportunity for philanthropy that can be a truly rewarding experience. This can be especially effective prior to birthdays and other gift-giving holidays, when your child is particularly aware that he is lucky to be receiving new toys very soon. I also recommend encouraging children not only to donate old toys but also to use some monetary savings to choose and purchase a new toy for a holiday drive or charity that collects new toys. When they are allowed to own the process, children are more likely to be enthusiastic about sharing their bounty.

It can be hard for children to part with these things; they're not always sympathetic to your decluttering goals. I suggest that you **create a holding zone.** Ask your child if it's okay to put away the toy in a bag or box in a closet, out of sight. If she misses the toy in a week, she can have it back (or sooner, if she's desperate), but I have yet to hear of any children asking for those old toys.

Often I find that the moms are more attached to the toys than their kids are. We get sentimental when our children move past one developmental stage and on to the next. We associate those trains, or LEGOs, or American Girl dolls with a particular time in our children's lives or with the person who gave the toy. When you find yourself clinging to a toy that your child doesn't care about anymore, remember that plenty of good times are still to come, and toys are just objects; they're not the memories that we associate with them.

Step 2: Design

The good news about designing the storage for your children's toys is that you likely don't need to go out and buy new furniture, and you certainly don't need to buy specialized furniture. Here's my list of the good and the bad in terms of storage:

RELY ON THESE

- **An ordinary bookcase with adjustable shelves.** Every household has one, and they truly are the most useful, flexible storage.
- **Labeled clear plastic drawers.** These are ideal because children can simply pull out the drawer of action figures, or whatever they're playing with at the moment, and then there's a defined location to return the drawer when they're done.
- **Matching bins.** These can work nicely when lined up on a shelf, and you can label the bin or the shelf itself.

ELIMINATE THESE

- ✄ **Toy chests.** I don't care if it's hand-painted and personalized or your grandfather carved it from a single tree that he chopped down himself; the toy chest is the devil. It is the worst possible black hole in which to store toys. The only play items that can be reasonably kept in a toy chest are stuffed animals or dress-up clothes. Otherwise, this is what you'll find in your toy chest: three LEGOs, two puzzle pieces, random game pieces, and other miscellaneous junk.
- ✄ **Plastic containers with lids.** I advise against these, especially for small children, because it can be frustrating for them to open and close lids. Even adults are less likely to put things away when lids are involved.

Step 3: Organize

Store the most often used toys at your child's eye level. If you have younger children whom you don't want getting into certain items unsupervised, place those items higher, where they can't be reached. Ideally, you have purged to a degree where you can arrange toys appealingly and in such a way that they're as visible and uncrowded as possible. Not only does that make the items more attractive to your child, it also makes them easier to put away.

Here's a list of popular toys and how best to store them:

- **Wooden blocks.** These are my favorite toys, bar none. They're beautiful, they're useful, they're fun. I've seen groups of children ranging from one to eighteen become mesmerized by building with them. An added bonus is that they are so easy to put away. Take a page out of the preschool rule book and devote the bottom shelf of a bookcase to blocks stacked and sorted by shape and size. Then step back and watch the magic unfold.

- **LEGOs and other building toys.** These often come in big cardboard boxes that are unwieldy to store. It's better to transfer them to labeled bins or closed containers. Plastic drawers or even lidded containers can work just fine, since these toys usually appeal to older children. And definitely don't forget to include the instructions!

- **Playmobils, Little People sets, and imaginative toys.** Often these toys combine a large play scene or building with lots of little pieces. You can place the large play scene on a shelf, then keep the smaller pieces in a labeled plastic drawer.

- **Plastic dinosaurs and animals.** Labeled bins are perfect for these items, especially if your child has a lot of them and uses them often.

- **Dolls and their related accessories.** Depending on the size of the doll, it can be kept on a shelf, and the accessories can go in a labeled plastic drawer. If furniture is involved, it can be arranged on a shelf or stored in a bin, depending on the size. Small accessories such as clothing can go in labeled plastic drawers.

Most important: **Avoid storing anything on the floor.** Unless it's a play table or other furniture-sized toy, it should have a place to reside—on a shelf or in a cabinet or closet.

Step 4: Maintain

In the play area—perhaps more than any other space in the home— the infrastructure that you design is the key to long-term organizational success. Once you've labeled and sorted items into labeled bins or boxes, your system is automatically enforced with other family members as well as caregivers, grandparents, and visiting children and their parents. Cleanup time is so much more effective as a result. There's no rush to toss something into the nearest bucket—the cars go with the cars, and the blocks go with the blocks. As with the art supplies we discussed earlier in this chapter, there are only two—slightly modified—**rules to instill in your children:**

1. Clean up after yourself.
2. Don't take out a new toy until you've put away the one you were just using.

Here are some other tips for maintaining order in the future:

- **The number of children you have, plan to have, and the genders of your children all help determine how you will purge your toys on an ongoing basis.** If you have a girl followed by two boys, you can eliminate a lot of the princess/doll/toy makeup things as your daughter outgrows them. But if you have a girl, then a boy, then a girl, you'll want to hang on to toys that girls tend to be drawn to for a longer time. Going forward, every three to four months, you should weed out the toys that your youngest child has outgrown, as well as the toys that are missing pieces or are broken.

- **Apply the twenty-four-hour rule to all party favors and similarly junky toys.** After twenty-four hours, bye-bye.

- **Before you invest in a very large toy that resides on the floor, ask yourself these questions:** 1) Do I have space for it? And 2) Will my child play with it every day, thereby justifying the fact that we will be living with this massive thing for the next two years? I suspect that at least half of all such purchases would be eliminated if parents thought through the answers to those questions.

- **Remember that you're in control of the clock.** You should end playtime well enough in advance so that cleanup can occur before everyone leaves or moves on to the next activity.

- **You have more control over gift giving than you think.** When my daughter, Rebecca, was three years old, someone gave her a birthday gift that trumpeted on the box cover: THREE HUNDRED INDIVIDUAL PIECES! I didn't even let the shrink wrap come off that box. Back it went to the store. You can do the same, but it's better to prepare gift givers in advance. If you don't want duplicates or gifts that clang and require batteries, then you have to tell grandparents and family members what your children *do* want—or, more important, what *you* want your children to receive. As children get older, I encourage grandparents in particular to give them experiences rather than things they don't need. Tickets to a show or sporting event are great gifts, and the side benefit is that grandparent and grandchild get to spend some wonderful quality time together. When all else fails, viva la gift card!

- **There's no point in arguing with an inveterate slob.** With regard to older children and teenagers, once you've established order and given them the tools they need to stay organized, the rest is up to them. Worst-case scenario, you can go to containment mode. Close the door to their hurricane-struck room (as long as they don't share it with another child), and establish the rule that they are allowed to be messy only in the areas that are theirs and theirs alone. In the public areas, your organizational rules are the law of the land.

Order Is Your Friend, Not Your Captor

When you're standing in your child's bedroom and you can't see the floor for all the toys and clothing, it may be hard to believe that he or she will ever fully buy in to the idea that less is more. There's hope, I promise you. Children can be conditioned! My own son, Matthew, is proof. When he was four years old and we were on our way to a kindergarten interview (yes, an interview for a four-year-old, don't even get me started on that crazy subject), I told him that I'd heard all the kids would be receiving a plastic firefighter as a gift at the end. Matthew immediately said, "Don't worry, Mom, I'll tell them we don't keep junky toys, and I'll throw it right away." Let me tell you, it took some convincing on my part to assure him that we could make an exception to that rule this one time.

Though the neat-freak apple doesn't fall far from the tree, even Matthew isn't perfect all the time. I'll make another little confession to you: My house is at its absolute messiest and most chaotic between the hours of four P.M. and eight P.M. That's when the twins come home from school and sports practice or bake cookies with friends (leaving the kitchen looking like a sugar bomb exploded). It's also when the textbooks are spread across the kitchen table, and I'm preparing for dinner at the same time.

Just because my home is well organized doesn't mean I don't have my moments of yelling, even if I know I shouldn't and that it doesn't help matters. Chaos happens to all of us. When it inevitably happens to me, I try not to stress about it when it's over. I have that luxury, for the most part, because a miraculous thing occurs in my home at eight P.M. every night. Suddenly, the house quiets down, and things revert to order. There's a place for everything, and everything gets returned to its place.

I think that's the key to sanity. It's not expecting ourselves (or our child or spouse) to be perfect every minute of the day. It is having the routines and plans in place that enable us to have a few serene, orderly hours in our home each day. It's also recognizing that if you take the time to return things to order just once a day, your life will be much, much easier tomorrow—and the day after that. I guarantee the next time your daughter can find her soccer equipment and your son knows exactly where the printer paper is for that report he has to finish for school, you'll see how your whole family can reap the benefits. They might even thank you for it someday. Hey, miracles happen.

5

BABY MAKES MORE
The Nursery

If you're reading this chapter, chances are you're either pregnant, thinking about having or adopting a baby, or you already have a nursery and you're trying to figure out how to make it a more organized place. If your children are out of the baby/toddler stage and you're not having any more, the last thing you want to read about is what to put in a diaper bag, am I right? So I won't be even slightly insulted when you moms of older children skip on by this chapter.

Thinking about organizing a nursery when you don't have a baby yet is a very different thing than trying to figure out how to improve the nursery you have. So this chapter is divided into two sections: The first is just for the newbies, and the second is for everyone.

Designing Your First Nursery

Since you're starting from scratch, there's no need to go through the four steps—my goal is to get you in the right frame of mind so you don't have to do as much purging and organizing later on. Here is my opportunity to brainwash you with "simplify, simplify, simplify" principles before you start camping out at Buy Buy Baby.

Isn't that a scary name for a store? They might as well call it Spend Spend Money. Don't get me wrong: It's a great store, an amazing resource, and I shopped there, too. But I do find that the *name* of the store captures an approach that too many of us take when a baby is on the way. Whether it's the nesting instinct or our acquisitive natures that drive us, we can all too easily be convinced that purchasing a bunch of stuff is an absolute necessity when having a baby. The truth is that the only things you need in order to take that baby home from the hospital are some diapers and a car seat. Okay, maybe that's an exaggeration, but only slightly.

You already know that I'm opposed to excessive accumulation, but as always, my attitude isn't solely due to my personal neat-freak ways. There's a genuinely good reason not to buy a ton of stuff for your baby before you absolutely need it: You don't know what you'll need yet, especially if you've never had a baby. For example, don't buy that expensive running stroller until you're sure you have the kind of baby—and the kind of schedule—that will enable you to use it. If you don't buy it now, you won't have to regret the purchase later.

Let's talk about what you need to acquire prior to your baby's arrival. What do babies do in the first few weeks of life? They eat and sleep, and in between they need to be kept dry and comfortable, and you're going to be carrying and pushing them places. That doesn't demand too much equipment.

Let's look at **the basic requirements:**

□ **A place for the baby to sleep and sheets to go with it.** I advise my clients not to think about a baby's sleep in stages, starting with a bassinet and moving on to a crib. It doesn't just cost more money to buy two separate items; it also creates greater and unnecessary complexity. The best plan is to purchase only a crib and sheets. As tempting as it may be, don't overdecorate the crib with bumpers, which aren't safe for the baby, or mobiles, which are an annoyance for you when you bang your head on them in the middle of the night.

□ **Bottles and accessories.** If you're breast-feeding, you'll need a pump and bottles, and if you're bottle-feeding, you'll need bottles and formula. Working-outside-the-home moms will need a separate bag for the pump. Bottles and pump accessories belong in a designated spot in the kitchen, preferably in a cabinet near the dishwasher or sink where the items will be washed.

□ **Changing table.** You can buy a piece of furniture called a changing table, but I'd much rather see you use a bureau you already have and place a changing pad on top. It's much more versatile in the long run and doesn't require another expenditure.

□ **Disposable diapers.** Some babies zip out of newborn-sized diapers very quickly; some skip that stage altogether. Just like adults, babies are built differently, so two eight-pound babies don't necessarily fit into the same diapers. You may find you prefer certain brands over others. This argues for buying one or two packages of newborn diapers at the outset (perhaps consider buying two different brands if you want to test them out). You could also buy a package of size 1 diapers, which fit eight-to-fourteen-pound babies, especially if you have reason to believe you're having a larger baby. You can't go wrong having a pack of size 1s, because most babies will stay at that stage for the first two to three months. One final piece of diaper advice: If you're tempted to stockpile size 1s when you see them on sale, just remember that brands do vary, and you may not know what type you and your baby will prefer.

☐ **Changing-table essentials.** Diaper cream and wipes are must-haves, and a stack of cloth diapers can come in tremendously handy for makeshift bibs, burping, and cleaning spit-up.

☐ **Clothing.** Your exact requirements will depend on the climate, but footed onesies are just about the best baby-clothing item ever invented—they're comfortable, easy to get in and out of, and no socks are needed! I will never understand the appeal of fussy baby clothes. The baby's not comfortable in them, and I'll tell you: Discomfort is not cute. Your baby will also need a hat, but since the hospital will send him home with one, you don't need to buy one in advance. I'm talking basics here, right?

☐ **Receiving blankets.** These are popular gift items, so it's a good idea not to go overboard. One or two soft blankets are all you'll need at the outset.

☐ **Car seat and baby carriers.** You need a car seat even if you don't own a car, because presumably, you will be taking a car or taxi home from the hospital. If you live in an area where you're in and out of the car quite a lot, you may want to purchase a car seat that drops right into its own stroller frame. In places where you're on and off public transportation, you'll want to choose an all-purpose stroller that folds and opens easily. You can purchase a sling or BabyBjörn at the start, but I've known parents of tiny babies who found that they couldn't use them, so bear in mind the likely size of your baby before you buy.

An important question to consider prior to buying washable items such as clothing and sheets is **what quantities do you need?** This is somewhat dependent on your proximity to laundry facilities. If you live in an apartment building with laundry facilities, or if your laundry is outside your building, then you may understandably want to stock up, especially since there can be a lot of dirty-diaper-induced clothing changes. But if your washer and dryer are no farther than your utility closet, kitchen, or basement, then there is no reason to stock up on more than three days of outfits (assuming three or four clothing changes per day, that works out to nine to twelve outfits). This might sound heartless, since buying baby clothes is so much fun, but if you overbuy and your baby grows quickly, he could easily outgrow items before he's ever worn them. Also remember that baby clothes are a popular gift, so you'll likely be receiving lots as presents.

There's a ton of baby-related stuff that I didn't mention in my list of basic requirements. That's why I call them *the basics*. I'll leave it to any number of baby guides, not to mention your pediatrician, to fill you in on the baby thermometers and other such items you should have in your arsenal. Anyway, I'm not worried that you're going to be undersupplied, because the world is so clearly conspiring to *over-supply* you.

Speaking of which, let me offer some **baby shower advice.** I'm all for gift registries. The whole concept makes good sense. When you're compiling your registry, think practically. Ask your friends and family to send you a list of the items that they found most useful, and while you're at it, go ahead and ask what they thought was a waste of money. Sometimes surprising and incredibly helpful items can come out of such lists, and often the cheapest drugstore items can be real finds. I have a friend who always gives the same set of colorful plastic cups to anyone having a baby. You can use them in the tub as a bath toy, and they're a great early stacking toy. They even work as teethers. The cost-per-use value is astounding. I also think one of the all-time best baby gifts is a favorite children's book or bookstore gift card. It's never too early to start a child's library.

We can't talk about gift giving without discussing **the evils of monogramming.** This will be a shot in the heart to sentimentalists everywhere, but my advice to all parents-to-be is to actively discourage gift givers from buying monogrammed presents, whether it's clothing or silver cups or wall art. Once something is initialed, it's impossible to return, even if it's a duplicate item or not to your taste.

Obviously, it won't be the end of the world if you end up with more baby supplies than you need. But it's good to cultivate a philosophy of restraint early on—once you develop a pattern of acquiring too much for your child, it's very hard to kick the habit. There is a big difference between what a baby *needs* and what you think might be nice.

Streamlining the Nursery

If your baby is several months or older, then you may already be faced with a nursery that is sliding into disorder. The older your baby gets, the more you receive and acquire, and there usually isn't a system in place to keep things organized. Let's separate the elements of baby care into categories and look at them one by one.

Diaper Stations

Step 1: Purge

I've already outlined in this chapter how few items you need for diaper changing. The concept of purging applies not only to what you keep on your changing table but also to the number of changing tables you have. I've been in households with multiple changing tables in various parts of the home, and they take up so much space—not to mention no one wants their living room to be dominated by diaper changing. Get rid of all but one changing table.

Steps 2 and 3: Design and Organize

As noted in the list of basic requirements, you don't need any specialized pieces of furniture. If you hang a shelf above the bureau, you can line up matching bins to hold diapers, wipes, and other essentials. If you change diapers elsewhere in the home, such as the living room, all you need is a foldable, portable diaper pad and some wipes. These can be placed in a decorative box to match your decor and then stowed away on a shelf.

Step 4: Maintain

This is easy as long as you follow the advice not to overpurchase supplies. Restrict your stocking up to the space allotted for your changing stations.

The Diaper Bag

You can often pick out the really experienced parents by their diaper bags. The newbies' bags are always the biggest, because God forbid they should forget something. They've got enough diapers for a week, a first-aid kit, board books, several changes of clothing, and on and on. Meanwhile, the experienced parents have one diaper and some wipes stuck in their purse or tote. They don't have a diaper bag.

You can find a happy medium between excessive and minimal. Before we go through the steps, let's list the ingredients of a streamlined, well-organized diaper bag:

- ☐ **Diapers.** A rule of thumb for moms of newborns is to pack one diaper for each hour you'll be out. Parents of older babies and toddlers should have a good idea of how many diapers their baby goes through. Pack the amount needed, plus two extra just in case.

- ☐ **Wipes.** You can pack a plastic travel case of wipes, but a lighter option for quick trips is to put a dozen or so wipes in a Ziploc bag.

- ☐ **Changing pad.** Often diaper bags come with a portable pad, but you can put one in any bag, and voilà, you've got yourself a diaper bag.

- ☐ **Hand sanitizer.** For those times when hand washing isn't possible.

- ☐ **Change of baby clothes.**

- ☐ **Bottle.** Unless you're breast-feeding.

If you're going out for a short time, the above is all you need to meet your baby's minimum requirements and to fend off any disasters.

If your bag is already an overstuffed mess, then use the above as your guide when you do Steps 1, 2, and 3. When you purge the diaper bag, as you did with your own purse in chapter 2, you should consider 1) what you use for your baby on a *daily basis,* and 2) what you absolutely need in a pinch. Anything else is excess and doesn't belong in the diaper bag. Remember, it isn't meant to be luggage. You're not going on vacation, you're headed out for a few hours. The bag itself doesn't need to be large—in fact, the more compact, the better. It just has to have sufficient pockets to keep things organized.

The key to step 4 is to make a habit of checking the bag after every outing. Replenish basic supplies, and remove anything you might have stuck in there during the day, such as soiled clothing.

Toys and Books

My attitude toward toy accumulation for babies and toddlers is the same as for older children—don't do it! It's far better to have a well-edited collection of quality toys than a landslide of stuff. It's my personal theory that we're building short attention spans into our children when we keep thrusting new games and toys at them. There's a reason that babies and young children love cardboard boxes, blocks, board books, spoons, and pots. Even babies know that simple is best.

Step 1: Purge

To begin, look around your home for all the duplicates. How many rattles does your baby need? Not as many as you currently have, I can pretty much guarantee. Books are just about the only item that you should have in large quantity. And you should try to weed out duplicates so you don't have five copies of *The Runaway Bunny*.

Steps 2 and 3: Design and Organize

Parents of babies and toddlers tend to keep baskets of toys on the floor, because so much of the small child's life is oriented toward that space. But big baskets of toys are the equivalent of the toy chest that I decried in chapter 4. They just encourage dumping and disorganization. Organizing toys by category into matching bins that can be stored on low shelves are a great option for young children and are just as accessible as the basket on the floor. There are many soft-sided and cloth choices available if you want something easy and safe for a toddler to carry around.

Step 4: Maintain

The best maintenance practice is to stay vigilant against overaccumulation. It's up to you as the parent to choose the items that will work best in your space. As mentioned in chapter 4, I always caution against toys that are so big they have to reside on the floor. Wait to purchase large items until you need them and are sure they will work for you. Why not try someone else's big-ticket item before you make the purchase yourself? Trust me, you'll hate that swing if you don't end up using it. Some babies love ExerSaucers, and they can be a great purchase, but you have to make choices—you can't have the ExerSaucer and the play table and the whatever-the-newest-thing-is if they're taking over your home. Or rather, you *can* have them all, but then your home will look like a Gymboree, and that's not a restful place for anyone, least of all your child.

Clothing

One of the wonderful things about having a baby is the generosity it brings out in others. In addition to all the clothing that we moms purchase for our children, we're being showered with adorable outfits from family members and friends, not to mention hand-me-downs. Before you know it, your baby's drawers and closets are exploding with so much clothing that she could compete with Lady Gaga for wardrobe changes.

Step 1: Purge

Since babies outgrow clothing at such a fast clip, it's important to regularly purge items that are too small. If you plan to have more children, make a clothing pile to store as hand-me-downs. If you aren't having more children, then bag these up for donation.

Steps 2 and 3: Design and Organize

Refer back to the advice in Chapter 4 for designing and maximizing children's clothing storage and for how best to organize items, particularly when you're storing multiple sizes.

Step 4: Maintain

The key to maintaining order is to remove items as soon as your child has outgrown them. Either store the outgrown clothing as hand-me-downs (see the next section), bag it up for donation, or put it into the trash if it's stained or too worn.

Hand-me-downs

People love giving hand-me-downs, because it seems like such a wonderful thing that the clothing they purchased for their own children won't go to waste when they're outgrown. But hand-me-downs are a very mixed bag. Though it sounds wasteful, the truth is that most hand-me-downs are more trouble than they're worth. You need to consider the following questions before you accept them:

- **How many years will you be storing the clothing before it's worn?** If the answer is more than one, just say no.

- **Do you have room to store the clothing?** If the answer is no, do yourself a favor and politely decline.

- **What condition is the clothing in, and does it appeal to you?** If you wouldn't buy those items for your child, then don't feel that you have to accept them.

- **Do you need to return the clothing after your children wear it?** *No backsies,* I always say. It's perfectly fair to say that you can't be trusted to keep track of those items and see that they get returned to their original owner.

- **Can you afford (and will you prefer) to buy new clothing?** If the answer is yes, then those hand-me-downs won't get worn and will only take up space in your closet.

- **Do your children have a similar body type?** If not, chances are they won't fit or flatter your child, so there's no point in accepting them.

ORGANIZING FOR TWINS

Having twins is a blessing times two, but it's also exhausting. I can't tell you how to get more sleep or grow extra sets of arms (or breasts), but I can tell you how to avoid turning your home into a baby supply store–cum–obstacle course: **Don't buy two of everything.** Twins are rarely doing the same thing at the same time, and they won't necessarily like the same things. You also don't want to build in to your twins the expectation that they must always have two of everything. We all have to learn to share. One thing that really helps with twins is **color coding.** This was especially important for me when my babies were newborns and I needed to know exactly how many ounces each was drinking. Having color-coded bottles made that a no-brainer. Which is exactly what you need when you have twin newborns!

The bottom line is: Whether you have to pay for something or the item is free, **don't bring home what you don't need and can't use.**

If you do have reason to accept or save children's clothes, hand-me-downs should be stored in bins labeled by gender, size, and season. For example, "size 3T girl fall/winter." And by all means, if that combination of events never seems to occur—the right gender, at the right time, at the right size—then off those hand-me-downs go to the next victim!

A Final Word of Advice

I'm going to get a little philosophical, so bear with me. The time when our children are babies and toddlers is very short, and it's precious. By all means, buy the things that will help your baby grow, develop, and laugh. Buy the adorable onesie not so much because your baby needs it but because you love it, and then treasure the picture you take of him wearing it. Try not to feel pressured into believing that you *have* to buy this or that, or that you're not a good mother if you don't buy the black-and-white flash cards for your three-month-old. The baby years are short. The child years are much longer. And if you want to get scared, just think of this: The high school and college years are coming. Don't buy so much for your baby now; save your money. You're gonna need it!

6

THE BARE NECESSITIES
The Bathroom and Linen Closet

Bathrooms are emotionally fraught areas of the home. And I'm not saying that because they're often the room where we spend the most time looking in the mirror. No, bathrooms are a tough subject because there's no other room that speaks so clearly to how much space we do—or don't—have. Think about it; The number of bathrooms in the home is probably the most significant piece of information in any real estate listing. It's one of the key ways to judge how well a space will work for a family.

No other room so directly impacts the traffic flow of our homes. Sure, I've been in homes where basically every member of the household had his or her own bathroom (and even in those homes, the bathrooms were cluttered!) The majority of us have to share that space. And most of us have delivered—or received—the occasional sharp elbow when we've tried to carve out our corner, which can make the already stressful morning rush even more intense. I know a lot of moms who wonder how it is that they end up getting the *least* amount of private time in their own bathrooms.

If you're among the many who would give a right arm for another bathroom, or even half a bathroom, then I empathize. Unfortunately, nothing in this book will tell you how to build an extra wing onto your apartment or house. But as with every other area of the house, I can tell you how to organize the space you have and the way you use it, so the time you spend in there is smoother and maybe even quicker.

In the second part of this chapter, we'll look at your linen closet or whatever extra space acts as your storage for towels and sheets. Finally, we'll address your backup supplies. By the end of the process, you might be amazed by how much more room you have . . . if you're willing to get rid of a few things. There's always a catch, isn't there?

The Bathroom

The bathroom is the last place that we should want clutter, but what we want and what we get are sometimes two different things. And it's our own fault! We're terribly self-indulgent when it comes to bathroom supplies. I have a client who is such a product hoarder that I told him if a natural disaster ever struck, I'd want to be evacuated to his house. The man has, no joke, at least a three-year supply of cold medicine.

The downside of all that accumulation is that bathrooms become hard to navigate and, even worse, hard to clean. The uneven surfaces of a crowded countertop attract dirt, moisture, soap scum, and toothpaste spray—yuck. Let's get rid of all the stuff that doesn't need to be there.

Step 1: Purge

The bathroom is a relatively small space, so at the start of your purge, you have the luxury of emptying the room the same way you would if you were doing a closet. Remove absolutely everything. It has the added benefit of giving you a chance to see what the room would look like without all the clutter, and it can be a good incentive to pare way down. Here's how to evaluate everything:

- **Put all reading material where it belongs.** I.e., *not* in the bathroom. Back issues of magazines should be recycled. Books should go on a shelf or on the bedside table if they are currently being read.

- **Make a pile of items that don't *need* to be in the bathroom.** Such as anything that is purely decorative. Toss anything you don't absolutely love and that detracts from the beauty and cleanliness of the room. Now put aside anything that remains in this pile until you get to steps 3 and 4.

- **Make a second pile of essentials that you use daily.** Shaving supplies, shampoo and conditioner, oral hygiene products, cleansers, etc. Now look at that pile and eliminate *all* duplicates. I've been in households where the moms felt it was important to provide their children with five different flavors of toothpaste. You are not the dentist; your children don't need a menu of options. It's understandable if family members have different shampoo and skin-care requirements, but there shouldn't be a variety of items that serve the same function—this includes different brands of volumizing shampoos, anti-wrinkle lotions, and cleansers. Pick the one item in each category that you like best and get rid of the rest. Eliminating unfinished items may sound wasteful, but if you won't use the contents, then you will eventually toss those items anyway.

- **Make a third pile of items that could be considered useful but are space hogs.** This includes decorative soaps, gift bottles of hand lotion that aren't used, and potpourri. Toss it all. You will *not* miss it.

- **Make a fourth pile of toiletries that are used only once a week or less.** Face masks, scrubs, etc. As you did with your essential toiletries, discard any duplicates and keep only those that you prefer and use. If you bought that hair treatment six months ago and you never make the time to use it, then you should toss it and learn a little lesson about yourself—hair treatments aren't for you. As for the items that remain: Keep these separate from your essential, frequently used items, because we now have the option of storing them outside of the bathroom. We'll discuss this more in steps 3 and 4.

- **Make a fifth pile of first-aid items and medicines.** Discard anything that expired, and make a list of items that you need to replace. Sort through boxes of bandages and consolidate by size and type. I often find five boxes of bandages that are empty except for two or three stragglers in sizes that are completely useless; consider your family's typical needs and toss any that don't fit the requirements. If you find that you don't make use of all the different sizes in assorted packs, then buy single-size boxes in the future.

- **Evaluate cosmetics and hairstyling products.** How many lip glosses of nearly matching shades do you need? Chances are one is your favorite, so why not keep just that? It makes getting ready in the morning so much easier when you don't have to spend one second of brain power deciding between the pinkish-brown lipstick or the brownish-pink one. As already noted, eliminate items that serve an identical purpose, such as multiple brands of hair spray.

- **Gather together the cleaning supplies.** There should be one area in the home for storing cleaning supplies—and the bathroom is not that place. If you have enough concealed storage in the bathroom, you could stash away *one* bottle of multipurpose spray cleaner and a microfiber cloth for wiping mirrors, chrome, and counters. Everything else should be reunited with your other household cleaning supplies in one central location (for more about that, see chapter 7).

- **Finally, purge the bath toys if you have them.** The bathtub often turns into the island of misfit toys—all the plastic stuff that you no longer want anywhere else in your home gets tossed in here. Get rid of anything that's unloved or mildewed and just plain gross. In terms of acceptable quantity, a small mesh bag hung from the showerhead or a bucket tucked in the corner should be sufficient to hold all the toys. When it overflows, you know it's time to purge again.

One final note on the subject of purging in the bathroom: It can be tricky to purge medical supplies, especially for moms. We feel great pressure to be ready for any and all possible medical emergencies. Rest assured, I'm not suggesting that you get rid of anything that your child really needs. To be extra certain, I asked Manhattan pediatrician Barbara Landreth, MD, to give **a list of the basics that all families with young children should have on hand:**

MEDICAL AND FIRST-AID SUPPLIES

- ☐ Digital thermometer
- ☐ Cotton swabs
- ☐ Oral dispensing syringe
- ☐ Tweezers
- ☐ Reusable hot/cold therapy packs
- ☐ All-purpose elastic bandage wrap
- ☐ Hypoallergenic bandages, assorted sizes
- ☐ Adhesive tape and sterile gauze pads, four-by-four

OVER-THE-COUNTER MEDICINES AND SALVES

- ☐ Aloe-vera gel
- ☐ Antifungal cream
- ☐ Triple antibiotic cream
- ☐ Hydrocortisone cream
- ☐ Petroleum jelly
- ☐ Antihistamine eyedrops
- ☐ Calamine lotion
- ☐ Ibuprofen suspension for fever or pain
- ☐ Acetaminophen suspension for fever or pain
- ☐ Diphenhydramine suspension for allergies and hives
- ☐ Normal saline nasal spray
- ☐ Oral rehydrating solution in single-dose packs
- ☐ Cola syrup for nausea/vomiting

Step 2: Design

The bathroom is a public space, so the organizing tools you use in open areas should be attractive and match your decor. Let's run down the types of storage and containers that can work well here:

- **Apothecary jars.** These are my absolute favorite for storing small items on an open shelf—cotton swabs, cotton balls, pony-tail holders, etc. They come in a variety of styles and sizes; just make sure they all match.

- **Plastic containers with drawers.** These are strictly for closed storage areas—in a cabinet under the sink, for example—and are excellent for related collections of items such as first-aid supplies.

- **Clear plastic drawer dividers.** These can be found in specialty organizing stores as well as home supply stores and can be dropped into any drawer or placed in a cabinet to help group things by category. My favorites come in various sizes, so you can customize them to your needs.

- **Dispensers.** Matching decorative dispensers for facial tissues, toothbrushes, and liquid hand soap pull together a bathroom's decor. You can cut down on visual clutter even more by using matching labeled pump-bottle dispensers for shampoo, condi-tioner, and liquid cleansers in the shower. These can be found at bath and beauty supply stores.

- **Trays.** I've already extolled the virtues of trays in other rooms in the house, and they work just as well here. A water-resistant tray on the bathroom counter can hold the soap and lotion dispenser. A tray on a shelf can hold a grouping of apothecary jars.

- **Bins.** If you lack for closed storage, an attractive bin on a shelf can be a good way of stashing a few backup rolls of toilet paper.

A plastic bin under the sink can hold a few essential cleaning supplies.

- **Free-standing storage column.** If you have the floor space and need the extra storage, consider investing in a narrow storage unit designed especially for the bathroom, which offers both open and concealed storage.

- **Mounted shelves.** If you need more storage space, see if there's a wall where you could install a single shelf or perhaps a narrow column of shelves.

- **Shower storage.** Recessed built-in shelves are the best space-saving storage, but if you don't have those, you can install a shelf directly into a tile wall. Alternatively, a caddy can be hung from a shower nozzle.

- **Towel hooks.** Towel bars take up precious wall space, and the towels inevitably look messy unless they're freshly laundered and folded. A few hooks on the back of the bathroom door are the most unobtrusive way of hanging towels. Even a row of hooks on a wall can look tidy when hung with matching towels (unmatched towels will always look messy). For more on managing your towel storage, see the linen closet section later in this chapter.

- **Shelf expanders.** These can be made of plastic or chrome and are good for keeping medicines visible in an eye-level cabinet. They're constructed like steps, so the rear-most items are higher than those in the front. Many are adjustable, so you can make them narrower or wider depending on your space.

Steps 3 and 4: Organize and Maintain

The guiding principle in organizing the bathroom should be Commandment 6: **Store things where you use them.** This means that many of the items below do not have to be kept in the bathroom. Whenever possible, move items to a linen closet, which tends to be more spacious—and dry—or to a bedroom. In the long term, maintaining order is as simple as always putting things back where they belong.

Let's evaluate things by category.

Medicine and first aid

The medicine cabinet isn't the best place for medicine for a number of reasons: 1) The bathroom is humid, and the temperature fluctuates. 2) You can't get to the medicine if someone else is using the bathroom. 3) The cabinet often isn't spacious enough.

An alternative solution for medicine is to set aside a spot in the linen closet or an area outside the bathroom. Organize the medicines with taller items in the back so that everything is visible and easy to find. Alternatively, you can use stackable plastic drawers for these items, grouping like with like.

First-aid items, as noted, can go in a labeled clear plastic drawer in closed storage in the bathroom; the drawer could also be placed in the linen closet. Sunscreens can be stored this way as well. The important thing is that everything is in one place and everyone knows where it is.

Shaving supplies and dental hygiene

Despite its name, the "medicine" cabinet is ideal for items that you typically use in a wet environment or that aren't sensitive to moisture, such as toothpaste and shaving cream.

Lotions and cleansers

Lotions, balms, and cleansers that you use every day can be stored in a medicine cabinet or in a drawer or other closed cabinet in the bathroom. While I prefer concealed storage, if your cleanser, lip balm, and lotions are well edited and attractively packaged, a few frequently used items could be grouped on a tray and stored on an open shelf.

Toiletries used once a week or less

If you have ample storage space in the bathroom after your purge, then your less often used scrubs and treatments can be stored the same way your lotions and cleansers are. However, if you lack for space, these items are best moved to the linen closet, where they can be stashed in a labeled container.

Hygiene tools

Tweezers, nail clippers, and other hygiene tools don't take up much space and get lost easily. Give them their own small bin in a medicine cabinet or divided space in a drawer.

Nail supplies

If you do your own manicures and pedicures, you likely have a host of products, from nail polishes and removers to files and specialized tools. You can store these items in a closed cabinet in a labeled drawer, or use a container to organize a smaller selection that's nice and portable.

Cosmetics, perfume, and hair products

If you have adequate closed storage, organize your makeup using dividers that can be tucked into a drawer or cabinet. The hair dryer (preferably with a cord that snaps up into the handle), brush, etc., should be concealed as well. If you don't use these items in the bathroom, then store them where you use them.

You can designate a drawer in a bedroom bureau for your hair dryer and makeup, using dividers to organize small items. If you have spare surface area in your bedroom, use an attractive lidded box to store makeup and some hair supplies. A tray on a bureau can hold a few perfume bottles and your brush. Now all you have to do is add some good lighting and an attractively framed mirror, and you have a calm spot to get ready in the morning. You can do the same for children who have their own morning routines.

Once you've found a place for everything you need, if you discover that you have room for a few decorative items in the bathroom—the ones you set aside as keepers when you were purging—you can return them now. Remember that less is more, and the items shouldn't make it harder to clean the space. Most of my clients find that they don't miss those extraneous things because a clean, clear space is so much more inviting.

The Linen Closet

Most of us store two kinds of items in a linen closet; 1) towels and sheets, of course; and 2) backup supplies of toiletries. Let's tackle those items one at a time.

Towels and Sheets

It always cracks me up when a client weeps over how little storage space she has and then she shows me how many linens she owns.

Considering how space-deprived many of us are, it's remarkable that we have whole closets devoted almost entirely to linens. So let's dig in there, purge, and I bet we can make room for a lot of the things that you no longer want to store in the bathroom.

Step 1: Purge

Before you can purge, you likely need to rethink how much of this stuff you need. I'm going to introduce you to a revolutionary concept, and you heard it from me first: **You need only two towels per person and two sets of sheets per bed.** That's it: two. One to use and one to wash. One on and one off. Simple. Now, because every rule must have an exception, I'm going to be extra generous and give you a few areas of flexibility:

- Keep one additional beach towel per family member, but only if they are actually used.
- Keep four pillowcases per pillow if you are in the habit of changing the cases more frequently than the sheets.
- If you have very young children, keep a third set of sheets for their beds to accommodate more frequent changes.
- If you have a guest bed or trundle bed, keep one set of sheets for it, and consider making it up with clean sheets; this way, you save space in the linen closet and you're always prepared. You can also keep a separate set of sheets for an air mattress if you have one.

This plan might seem extreme at first. Clients often say, "Won't the sheets and towels wear out and get grungy if I use them over and over?" Well, how often do you change your sheets—once a week? If you alternate your sheets, then you're washing each set of sheets two to three times per month. Your sheets aren't going to wear out so quickly on that schedule. And when your towels start to look worn, guess what? You can toss them and buy more!

Now that you know the basic rules, here is what to do:

- Obviously, get rid of excess towels and sheets. Sheets can be donated if they are in good condition.
- Toss all themed sheets sets if your child has outgrown them.
- Discard random items—single towels, sheets, or pillowcases that don't match anything else.
- Be strict about tablecloths and other table linens. First, make sure that you're keeping only linens that fit the tables you have. Then ask yourself if you have far more than you need. Do you have ten tablecloths but you use a tablecloth maybe once a year? Pick the one or two that are nicest and donate the rest.

Step 2: Design

The extra space you've created with purging will mean that you can stack sheets according to size and **label the shelf underneath.** You can do the same thing with linens if you have many of them. Towels need no special infrastructure.

Truly, the best design tip for the linen closet is to properly fold what you have. Things look tidier that way, and they take up less space on the shelf. So here are the **rules for folding:**

- The fold of the towel, sheet, or tablecloth should always face out.
- Fold each item uniformly and to uniform sizes—all sheets folded to the same dimensions. This holds true for all towels, etc.
- If your shelves are widely spaced, you may want to fold your towels in vertical thirds before folding them in horizontal

thirds (this way they will stack taller as opposed to wider). Or you may prefer to fold them in half and then in thirds. Either way, fold each towel the same so that they stack uniformly.

Let's face it: Most of us can fold a towel. The real killer is **the fitted sheet.** Once you get the hang of it, I promise it's not as dastardly as it seems:

1. Fold it in half.
2. Tuck one pair of fitted corners *inside* the other.
3. Fold it in half again, and once again fold one fitted corner inside the other. Now you have a rough rectangle.
4. Lay the sheet on a flat surface and slightly fold over the edge that isn't perfectly even to make a tidy rectangle.
5. Now you can finish folding, and voilà—it doesn't look half bad!

Steps 3 and 4: Organize and Maintain

Towels are best stored in the linen closet, but another option for sheets is to keep them in the bedrooms, since that's where you use them. A spare bureau drawer can easily fit one set of backups. If the linen closet is the only option for sheet storage, that's fine—the key to keeping order now and forever is to follow the two-per-bed/person rule.

Backup Supplies

If buying in multiples is a big problem in the bathroom, then buying in bulk—especially from big-box stores and price clubs—is the biggest issue in the linen closet. We're drawn in by the idea that we're saving money if we buy the three-pack of cotton swabs or a thirty-two-ounce bottle of conditioner. But if it takes us years to go through all those swabs or months to go through that bottle, then it's not justifying the space it's taking up. Even if you would go through a twenty-four-pack of toilet paper in a little less time, you must ask yourself if you should be devoting an entire shelf in your home to toilet paper.

Space isn't the only issue. Expiration dates can also be a problem. Most skin-care products feature a number of months by which the item should be used once opened (six months, two years, and so on). Sunscreen must be used within one year of opening, but in one client's apartment, I found—no exaggeration—seventeen bottles. We all want to be prepared, but it's counterproductive if a good portion of your sunscreen is growing less potent by the day. The same is true for over-the-counter medications. Before you buy that thousand-count bottle of ibuprofen, ask yourself: How long will it take my family to go through it?

There are three main reasons that my clients buy such large quantities of staple items:

1. **The Boy Scout creed—be prepared!** There's a fear lurking in the hearts of so many of us: What if I run out of shampoo/ soap/toilet tissue? This is when you have to remind yourself that you do not live in Antarctica, and you can easily replenish when supplies run low.

2. **I don't know if I have it, so I'll just buy more.** How many times have you been in the price club and wondered if you have enough toothbrushes or dental floss or toilet paper? You're not sure, but you decide to buy more anyway, to be on the safe side. Then you get home and find out you already have plenty of toothbrushes but what you really needed was

toothpaste. The obvious solution is to check your inventory and make a list before you go. It's also wise to keep one central list for all your shopping, especially since so many stores sell food and non-food items now. You could even keep a running list on your smartphone, so you always have it with you.

3. **If I buy it now, then I won't have to buy it later.** It seems like such a time-saver to buy in multiples. But it's no time-saver when you have so much stuff in your linen closet that you can't find what you need when you need it.

So now let's reduce and bring some order to all those backup supplies you've got. This process should be easier now that you know better!

Steps 1, 2, and 3: Purge, Design, and Organize

First toss all expired items and anything your family is tired of or doesn't use.

Now, how to design the best storage for what remains? The linen closet is a great place for stackable plastic drawers, as noted earlier in this chapter. You can group cold medicines, sunblock, pain relievers, bandages, and first-aid ointments, etc., each in its own drawer, and label the drawers accordingly.

Backup supplies and less often used items that are too large for drawers can be lined up on the shelves of the linen closet, grouping like with like (hair products, paper products, etc.). If you store like with like, you reduce the chance that you'll buy more than you need, because you can quickly scan the shelf to see what you have and what you might need to replenish.

Step 4: Maintain

The bottom line: **Let a store be a store.** You don't have to turn your home into a warehouse. It's great to make sure you have the necessities, and it's fine to add on a few of the extras that you love. Realize that if you don't want your linen closet to burst at the seams, then you have to be choosy about what you store. Be realistic about what your family uses, and how much, and then trust that if you are ever desperate for more shampoo, there's a store out there that can help you with that.

Spick-and-Span

The most basic requirements for a bathroom and linen closet are cleanliness and order. A sparkling bathroom is a pleasure, and a tidy linen closet is the definition of practicality. I have an even greater goal for you in streamlining these two areas: The more you're able to reduce excess, the more usable space you're able to create. I have managed to clear so much space in a linen closet that I was able to transform several shelves into toy storage. In one case I was able to empty an entire linen closet and transform the space into a home-office nook. Though you might not be able to do that, you can probably designate a portion of your linen closet for storage of other items—household tools, cleaning supplies, whatever you lack space for elsewhere. Hey, you might even have room for that jumbo pack of toilet paper you brought home from the price club. Sure, I told you not to do that, but I'm nothing if not realistic!

7

CLOSE YOUR EYES AND
SHUT THE DOOR
The Utility Closet

Cleaning supplies. Tools. Laundry. What do all these things have in common? None of these items is considered particularly attractive. And while there are some of us who genuinely *like* to clean, fix things around the house, and launder clothing, for most of us there is one unappealing word that encompasses those activities: chore.

Maybe that's why we pay so little attention to how we store those things. Or maybe it doesn't occur to us that there's a pay-off to organizing them in a user-friendly way. Whether you clean and fix because you have to or because you enjoy it, a well-thought-out storage area can make those tasks far more pleasant.

In fact, it was something as unsexy as a laundry room that sparked my first and only case of apartment envy. I'm in and out of my clients' apartments all the time, and I've been in some astoundingly beautiful homes. But I'm not the kind of person to crave what other people have—which is a good thing, considering my line of work. However, there was one day that the green-eyed monster of jealousy emerged in me. That was when I went into an apartment where they had *two* washers and *two* dryers in their own laundry room. Be still my heart.

Obviously, that was beyond luxurious. Most of us are lucky to have a designated closet for those less attractive items, and very few homes have separate places for cleaning, laundry, and tools. Often the vacuum cleaner goes in the front closet because that's where there's space. The cleaning supplies are spread all over the house. And dirty laundry ends up everywhere from the hallway to the bottom of a closet. To make matters worse, there are all kinds of items such as luggage, shoe polish kits, extension cords, and other random necessities of life that have to share the real estate. In other words: Chaos rules. But you don't have to let that happen.

Before we dig in, let me pause and address space constraints and what they means to each of us. I've noted here and elsewhere that some of my clients have tons of space, yet they manage to overfill their square footage. Still, it's true that the less space you have, the far greater your organizational challenges are. Apartment dwellers are the most restricted of all. Even modest houses will have more square footage than the average apartment. Larger houses might have a basement and an attic as well as a mudroom.

This chapter is assuming certain space limitations that may not exist in every home. Since I live in New York City, the capital of cramped living conditions, I have geared my advice toward readers who share that concern and who may store things that properly belong in a utility closet in tight conditions and in any number of locations in the home. You might not have the same issues. If you have a separate laundry room with a shelf right above your washer and dryer, then it's easy to figure out where you'll put your detergent. While the specific advice in this chapter won't be equally applicable to everyone, the principles remain the same and are universally helpful: Less is more. Store like with like. Eliminate excess. No matter what size your home is, that's sound advice.

Steps 1–4: Purge, Design, Organize, and Maintain

As with the front closet, the utility closet is a catchall for a whole variety of items. So we're not going to try to take steps 1 through 4 for every single one. Rather, let's look at each category of items that you store and apply the steps and commandments where and how they make the most sense.

Luggage

We tend to keep a hodgepodge of luggage from all stages in our lives, which can consume an awful lot of space. A **purge** is important here.

- **Pull out everything** in the home that you travel or cart stuff with.
- If you didn't already go through this step in chapter 2, **get rid of all your piles of freebie tote bags,** with the exception of those that you use *often* for groceries and other kinds of hauling.
- **Toss any random duffel bags and travel bags** that you've acquired over the years but don't use anymore.
- **Toss all broken luggage**—anything ripped, or with a damaged wheel or zipper.
- **Consider the maximum number of pieces your family would need on a trip**—and the pieces they actually use—and that's the amount you should keep, no more.

In terms of **organization and storage location,** if you have a frequent business traveler in your home, then it makes sense to keep his or her carry-on in a handy location. That could be a closet shelf—preferably at an accessible height—or on the floor of the front coat closet, if you have the room. All other less often used baggage can be stored inside of each other: A carry-on bag can be tucked inside a larger suitcase, and so on. These bags can be placed on the uppermost shelf in a closet. Even better, if you have a storage unit, attic, or basement, keep them there.

Tools

I've had clients who didn't know the difference between a flathead and a Phillips head but who gave over prime cabinet and closet space to huge boxes of tools, not to mention power equipment. I'm not going out on a limb by saying that it's usually the husband who accumulates in this area, and men can get a little insulted if we wonder when they last used that circular saw.

Tools can be aspirational items—sometimes they speak more to the kind of life we'd *like* to lead than to the life we do lead. Of course, if you have an incredibly handy member of the household, then by all means let that person keep all the tools he/she desires; they're worth their weight in gold. The rest of us less handy types should **stick to the basics and purge anything else.** So what are the basics?

Though I'm a minimalist by nature, even I was pleasantly surprised when I spoke with Andrew Liebhaber, president of Liebhaber Construction in New York City, and he told me how few tools the average person needs. Regardless of the size of the home, he recommends that **if you're starting from scratch, you should simply purchase a good-quality complete tool set,** which you can find at a home center for as little as fifty dollars. Remove the tools from the plastic case and put them in a toolbox that will accommodate everything. If you already have a vast array of tools, here's a list of those Liebhaber considers basic and worthwhile. You can **give away anything that's not on this checklist:**

- ☐ 16-oz. hammer
- ☐ Two slotted screwdrivers (small and medium)
- ☐ Two Phillips screwdrivers (small and medium)
- ☐ Slip joint, needle-nose, and diagonal pliers
- ☐ Ten-inch torpedo level
- ☐ Sixteen-foot tape measure
- ☐ Adjustable wrench

If you have a loved one with a craving for power tools, Liebhaber says that the most versatile is a cordless drill, which can be used for drilling holes as well as driving screws. He also recommends including a standard flashlight in your repair arsenal, as well as a four-foot stepladder. His favorite home repair tool of all? A roll of duct tape.

Once you've organized everything in a toolbox, you can store it on an upper shelf in a utility closet, linen closet, or a kitchen cabinet if that's where you have more storage space.

Extension Cords

These don't need to take up prime real estate. They're not emergency items. Not to mention, how many of them do you really need? It's fine to have a few backups, but more aren't necessary, and they'll just end up in an unmanageable snarl. After you've purged, wind each extension cord neatly and wrap it with a twist tie so it doesn't unravel. Then place them all in a labeled plastic container that can be stacked on a shelf in the same area where you store tools.

Lightbulbs

First purge the bulbs and make sure you're not storing specialized bulbs for lamps or overhead lighting that you no longer have. Make sure all bulbs are working, and make a note to purchase backups of any that you don't have. Finally, be sure to keep all your bulbs in one place in the home—**remember Commandment 5, to store like with like, and designate a place for everything.** Put all of the bulbs in a labeled plastic drawer or labeled and lidded plastic container and stash them in a utility closet or linen closet. If you have a lot of shelving in a public space, you could put the bulbs in a decorative box that matches your decor and keep them there—no one outside the family needs to know that you've got bulbs in there.

Emergency Kit

We don't often use this, but it needs to be easily retrievable—that means eye level or below, not buried. A kitchen cabinet or linen closet is a good option. I keep mine in the laundry room. A basic emergency kit should have:

- ☐ Two flashlights (in addition to the one you keep with your tools) with backup batteries
- ☐ Nonelectronic rotary phone
- ☐ Battery-operated radio

You can find government guidelines for more elaborate emergency kits, but those are the basics. Keep all items grouped together in a labeled container.

Batteries

You want these accessible, especially for those times when you're in the middle of a document and your mouse dies. A labeled clear plastic box, preferably with a drawer for easy retrieval, works well, and they can be stored on a shelf in a cabinet or closet, preferably as close as possible to eye level. Alternatively, as with lightbulbs, you can store them on an open shelf in a living area in an attractive covered box. The key is to keep them all in the same place so you always know where they are.

Shoe-cleaning Supplies

This whole category of items causes me to roll my eyes. Buried in some closet in a client's home, I regularly find a box of ancient shoe polish and rags that are stiff with age. When I ask when these items were last used, the client can rarely remember. Be realistic. If you want to be able to touch up your shoes, most likely you can get by with one of those convenient instant-polish sponges. They close up in their own case, and there's no mess or drips so you can safely tuck them in the linen closet. For anything more serious—such as waterproofing and salt stains—the vast majority of people will seek out the help of a cobbler. And that is why the box of shoe polish is invariably so old and crusty! Time to purge. If there are items you actually use, then store them in a labeled plastic container in the linen closet or where you keep your shoes. Personally, I don't keep any of this stuff—a shoe shine at the cobbler is one of the cheapest ways in this world to feel like a king. It's well worth the occasional five dollars to me.

Laundry and Supplies

If your washer and dryer are in the home, then of course it makes sense to store the detergent right nearby. If you take your laundry outside the home, you might want to store the detergent right inside your laundry bag, hanging on a hook in the front closet.

Here are some tips for how to design infrastructure and maintain the right habits to keep you organized:

1. **Store stain remover where you take off your clothing.** My children have been trained to pretreat their clothes from a very young age, and we keep the stain remover under the sink in the bathroom.

2. **Keep a covered hamper in the bathroom for dirty laundry.** If you're planning a renovation soon, then the best hamper is built in and has a liner that you can slip in and out. If you don't have room for a hamper in the bathroom, keep one in each bedroom—in either case, it should match the decor. Some hampers have dividers for separating whites and colors, but that's not a necessity—all sorting can be done when you're ready to do the laundry.

3. **Get rid of your full-size ironing board.** Opt for a half-size board that can be perched on a table and then stashed away much more easily.

4. **Hand-launder as you go.** I don't know anyone who enjoys hand-laundering clothing, but it becomes a truly heinous task when you allow it to pile up. Definitely don't keep a separate hamper for hand washables—that's just an out-of-sight-out-of-mind way to let it accumulate. Instead, hand-launder anything that needs it the moment you take it off. I keep some of my hand-washing detergent under the sink so I can drop whatever I've just removed into some soapy water, rinse it, and in two minutes I'm done.

5. **Dry cleaning goes into a separate matching hamper.** I use two different dry cleaners. My husband, Jeffrey, goes through five dress shirts a week, and he and I both accumulate dry cleaning, so I send his work shirts to a dirt-cheap place to be laundered, and I send our dry cleaning to another. Truth be told, I keep a spreadsheet—that lists what shirts went to the dry cleaner, with a spot for me to check off that they all came back—but that may be too much information! To keep things a bit simpler, once you've designated a single hamper for dry

cleaning, the best rules of thumb for streamlining the process are:

- **Remember Commandment 2: Routines work.** For example, if you always take your dry cleaning or shirts to the cleaners on the same day on your way to work, and you always pick them up on the same day after work, then you can plan accordingly and you'll never have to wonder where that blouse or suit is.

- **Keep your own stash of stain stickers.** Ask your dry cleaner for a roll. Then you can put one on that blouse or tie the moment you take it off, while you still remember where the stain is.

Shopping Bags

Many of us keep absurd quantities of department and specialty store shopping bags in all sizes—big ones, tiny ones, and most of them useless. If you have already kept an edited quantity of tote bags for shopping trips, then ask yourself what purpose you expect the rest of these to serve. When was the last time you used any of them? I'm going to hazard a guess: rarely or never. If you occasionally use them, then keep a small handful, but only if you have a place for them—folded up inside each other and hung on a hook in the utility closet, or folded flat and stored in a labeled, lidded plastic container and placed on a shelf or in a kitchen cabinet. Recycle the rest.

Cleaning Supplies

In a lot of homes, I see cleaning supplies stored in three different places—under the sink in the kitchen, under the sink in the bathroom, and in a utility closet. As I noted in the bathroom chapter, it's fine to keep one bottle of all-purpose spray there. You can do the same in the kitchen if that's not where you already store most of your cleaning supplies. The problem is when we can't keep track of what we have or where it's stored, because we have it in so many different places. This results in a lot of disorganization and duplication.

You should have one central location for your cleaning supplies other than the exceptions I just noted. A plastic caddy is a great way to store cleaning supplies, since it can be carried from room to room. The caddy should be stored where you have the most space—under the sink in the kitchen or in a utility closet. Of course, items such as brooms will have to go in a closet. For these I recommend a hook, if the item has a loop on the end, or you can also purchase a rack from a home supply or hardware store to mount on the back of a door.

Wherever you keep your supplies, don't overbuy. Many of my clients have way more cleaning supplies than they need. Sometimes it's because they're buying in bulk (as noted in chapter 6, this approach is definitely not recommended). Often it's because they've fallen into the trap of thinking they need too many specialized products. **You need only a few, so here's a checklist:**

- ☐ Laundry detergent, bleach, stain pretreater
- ☐ Glass cleaner
- ☐ Multipurpose spray cleaner (if you store your cleaning supplies outside of the kitchen, you may want to keep one extra bottle under the kitchen sink as well as one under the bathroom sink)
- ☐ Microfiber cloths are excellent for polishing wood furniture and making stone countertops gleam, as well as for cleaning chrome fixtures, mirrors, and stainless-steel appliances. Plus, they're washable and last forever. Score one for the environment.
- ☐ Cream cleanser for tubs, sinks, and toilet bowls
- ☐ Wood cleaner for furniture
- ☐ Vacuum cleaner

- ☐ Broom and dustpan
- ☐ DustBusters are great for quick cleanups of food crumbs and other dry spills, but if you already have a vacuum cleaner, you can do without.
- ☐ Floor wipes attach to a handle for use on wood and hard floors. I vastly prefer them to mops, which I think just shove dirt around. The wipes also eliminate the need for a separate bottle of floor cleanser.

Electronics and Chargers

In any home, go to the spot where charging takes place. Often it's the kitchen. There you'll find a tangle of cords on the counter and an even bigger tangle of chargers stuffed in a drawer. It's likely that half of those chargers belong to electronics you no longer have. Because there are so many and it's such a mess, instead of figuring out which are the right chargers, you keep all of them.

It's time to purge, design, and organize that tangle. Identify which chargers go with which phones and equipment. Then take out your labeler and wrap a label around one end of each. Use a twist tie to make a nice loop of each charger (no balled, knotted-up cords). Get some drawer dividers and plop each into its own compartment. Easy, tidy. Why would you want to do it any other way?

Once you've made sure all your phones and cameras have chargers and all of your other electronics work, all those extra mystery cords and chargers should go bye-bye. Worst-case scenario, if you make a mistake and toss the wrong one, chargers are not irreplaceable. Chances are you won't make a mistake. I've never been in a household with too few chargers—it's always the opposite.

The Junk Drawer

No one should have a junk drawer.

Go ahead, tell me I tricked you. You thought I was going to tell you how to tidy it. Let me reassure you: You don't need it. If you follow the four steps—**purge** the detritus, **design** storage, **organize** like with like, and **maintain** that order—then you'll realize that nothing in your house deserves to be called a junk drawer. You don't *keep* junk, you keep things you need. And each of those things has its place. Maybe you have a drawer in your kitchen where you keep your labeled chargers. And maybe in that same drawer you have a slotted organizer with backup house keys, birthday candles, toothpicks, and matches.

That, my friend, is *not* a junk drawer. That is a thing of beauty!

8

THE LAND OF MILK AND HONEY
The Kitchen and Pantry

We've all been raised to think that abundance is a good thing, particularly when it comes to food. More is better, right? So we don't have three kinds of cereal, we have fourteen. This is no exaggeration; I've witnessed it. Why get just one bag of English muffins, we reason, when the big-box store sells packs of four? And if our family really likes that brand of potato chip or cracker or jam, then why not stock up? I swear, some pantries look like the household is gearing up to feed the local fire department.

I don't need to tell you that all this accumulation is excessive—you know it is. But old habits die hard, especially in the kitchen. For many moms, food seems so essential and basic to a family's survival that we feel justified in our accumulation. That doesn't go just for the food, it also goes for utensils, appliances, pots and pans, and on and on. We pack it in and rarely throw any of it away, except the food we've over-purchased and could never consume by the expiration date.

The first task in evaluating your kitchen is to evaluate your life: Who are you as a person and a family? Do you cook a lot, a little, or not at all? Do you have people over for dinner? Do you bake? What other activities do you use your kitchen for?

In answering these questions, it's essential to be realistic. The question isn't, would you *like* to cook a lot—the question is, *do* you cook a lot? Often we arrange and acquire for our kitchen not based on who we are but who we aspire to be. There's nothing wrong with aspiring, if that's what genuinely gives you joy. If you're taking a baking class because you've always wanted to make pastry, then I'll give you a pass on the baking equipment around. And if you love to bake and you use all that specialized equipment, then wonderful (and can I come over?). But if rolling out pastry dough is the equivalent of walking on hot coals to you, and that rolling pin mocks you or lands on your feet with a thud every time you open your cabinet door, then why are you keeping it around? There's no law on the books that says you have to make pie or they'll take your children away from you. Think how much less pressure (and self-ridicule) you'll feel when you get rid of the stuff you don't use and focus on the things you do like to do. You wouldn't keep a ball gown in your closet if you weren't Cinderella. So if you never serve banquets, why do you have that huge coffee service? You get the idea.

The same thing goes for figuring out what you do in the kitchen aside from food preparation. In keeping with my "store it where you use it" philosophy, I have no problem with keeping nonkitchen items in the kitchen. If that's where you charge your phones because the counter and multiple electrical outlets make it most convenient, then that makes sense to me. If it's where your children do their homework, then maybe it's also the best place to sign the permission slips. Again, be realistic. The kitchen can do a lot, but it can't do everything at least not well. Figure out what you need your kitchen to do and what you want to do there, and make the space accommodate your needs and your life.

Step 1: Purge

There are a lot of different items in the kitchen. Let's break them into categories.

Small Appliances

These are the first things I like to purge in a kitchen. They're such counter cloggers, and they seem to reproduce like rabbits in a cage. I have been in kitchens where there were multiple sizes of food processor, as well as a stand mixer, hand mixer, immersion blender, waffle iron, panini maker, ice cream maker, bread maker, sno-cone maker, espresso maker, bread toaster, toaster oven, and multiple juicers. In many cases, these items were gifts that seemed fun. After their first and only use, they became a burden to store.

It's time to take out all of the items (i.e., anything portable with a plug) and evaluate them one by one. Ask yourself these questions:

1. **Do I own another appliance that can be used for this purpose?** For example, do you need the old-fashioned toaster as well as the toaster oven? If you have all the room in the world, maybe you can keep both. But who among us has all the room in the world? Keep the one that serves the most purposes.

2. **How often will I use it?** An espresso maker is a lovely idea, but if you use it only once a month—or never—then it isn't adding to your quality of life.

3. **Am I really going to throw a fondue party/ice cream social/ panini picnic?** These items are the easy pickings—they're

just taking up space. This also goes for those appliances that you used at one point in your life, but you just aren't that into anymore—the juicer when you were obsessed with juicing, or the bread maker when it seemed like the greatest thing ever.

One final caveat: There are those appliances that you might use infrequently but are absolutely essential when you do use them. If the item is small and light and you can tuck it away, great. Often, however, the essential but not so frequently used item is the big food processor or the stand mixer that won't fit in any drawer. Luckily, many are attractive and coordinate well with the kitchen, so if one of these heavy guys is tucked into the corner of your counter, ready for service, I'm okay with that. It's true that we're more likely to use the items that we see. Unless we're talking about a sno-cone maker.

Tools, Utensils, Pots, and Pans
Most of us have more than we need. Partly, this is the fault of all those wedding gifts—the pot-and-pan assortments that include sizes that aren't useful, and the knife blocks with far more knives than you or can keep sharp. As we marry (and remarry) and combine households, couples often put all their stuff together without weeding out the duplicates. The result is a kitchen with five wooden spoons, four spatulas, and two ladles. You can argue with me about the wooden spoons, but I swear to you: No one needs more than one ladle.

Ironically, we amateurs pile up on the kitchen supplies, but professional chefs are all about economy. Dalia Jurgensen, pastry chef for Brooklyn's Michelin-starred restaurant Dressler and author of the memoir *Spiced,* is a case in point. I asked her what she uses in her kitchen at home—not just once in a while but constantly—and she also told me what she finds to be a big waste of time.

RELY ON THESE

- ☐ **Microplane.** For grating hard cheeses, citrus zest, whole nutmeg.
- ☐ **Heat-safe rubber spatula.** For everything: scrambled eggs, risotto, soup, folding batters.
- ☐ **Hand blender.** (Also called an immersion blender or stick blender), preferably with a chopping attachment and detachable wand for easy cleaning. For smoothies, soups, baby food, and loose purees. The chopping attachment is great for small jobs (no need to drag out the big food processor for a handful of nuts).
- ☐ **Nonstick omelette pan.** Really the only thing to use for eggs; just make sure you get the best quality available, and one that's labeled "green," which means that the chemicals stay in the coating, not your food.
- ☐ **Y-shaped peeler.** The only kind chefs use, because it's easier to handle than straight peelers; shaped like a slingshot and costs about three dollars.
- ☐ **Tongs.** Any chef will tell you that this is an all-time favorite tool.
- ☐ **Fine sieve.** For straining homemade stock and creating silky-smooth purees, and it can double as a colander.
- ☐ **Knives.** All you really need are a quality chef knife (worth investing some money in) and some small serrated paring knives that cost about six dollars at a restaurant supply store.
- ☐ **Pots and pans.** The heavier, the better, both for conducting heat and for easier cleaning—definitely worth the investment. A good assortment would include a Dutch oven (for stovetop stews as well as oven braises and roasts); a sauté pan that can double as a frying pan; an eight-quart or larger stockpot (*if* you make soup and broth); and one-quart, two-quart, and four-quart pots.

- ☐ **Food processor.** Okay, this isn't an everyday necessity, but when it's needed, nothing else will do.
- ☐ **Stand mixer.** Again, you might not use it every day, but if you bake, it is essential. If you don't, then skip it.
- ☐ **Scale.** If you're serious about baking, this is the *only* way to measure.

DON'T BOTHER WITH THESE

- ✂ **Hand mixer.** If you have an immersion blender and a stand mixer, then you don't need this.
- ✂ **Onion goggles.** They're supposed to keep your eyes from watering when cutting onions, but they're just silly.
- ✂ **Fancy/complicated wine openers.** They're not easier or faster. And often they're huge! A simple wine key is the best and cheapest.
- ✂ **Avocado knife.** Or any knife that has a specific purpose. Just use an ordinary knife! This level of specialization is a total waste of money.

Baking Items

They can take up a lot of space in cabinets, and they vary in size and shape, so they're hard to consolidate neatly. Pull out everything you have and evaluate what you use. Aim to have items match in brand and style so they stack better—have the same kind of measuring cup, the same kind of cake pans, etc.

Let's go through a list of **common baking items and the quantities you should keep:**

- ☐ Two sets of measuring cups and spoons
- ☐ Two muffin pans
- ☐ Four cookie sheets—two to go in the oven, and two waiting to go in

- ☐ Three round standard-sized cake pans—if you make three layer cakes; if you make only two layer cakes, then keep that many
- ☐ Two bread pans

And here are two things that you should avoid keeping altogether:

- ✂ Specialty pans that you used once years ago for a particular recipe and never again
- ✂ Cookie-cutter sets take up a lot of space, and invariably, there are shapes that don't work. If you make shaped cookies, keep a few shapes that you like and use.

Dishes

As noted, duplication and mismatching are two of the biggest reasons for cabinet disorganization. **If your dishes all match, they will look more pleasing on the shelf,** and they will also stack neatly. If you have all one kind of dish, then it's easier to evaluate whether you have the right quantities. What is the maximum number of people you feed at one time? That's the number of dishes you should have, no more. Also purge any chipped plates, since you don't use them.

Take the same approach to glasses, cups, and mugs. Calculate your needs and get rid of the rest. Bear in mind that if you have all one kind, they will look much tidier when lined up in the cabinet. For more about what to do with never-used china or the silver service handed down to you from a relative, see chapter 11.

A word about children's dishes and cups: Most homes have more plastic plates and bowls than they ever use, and the assortment is totally haphazard. I recommend that my clients avoid the cutesy theme plates and calculate how many child-size plates, utensils, and cups they need, then buy matching sets. Sturdy solid-color melamine lasts a long time, looks nicer, and stores well. (Just remember that no plastic dish or cup should be used in the microwave.) As for sippy cups, color-coding for your children can work well to avoid arguments, but buy only one brand so you don't have a mismatched jumble of tops and bottoms. Moreover, you probably don't need more than four per child. And by all means, once your children have graduated to real dishes, then dump all the plastic. I recently organized a kitchen for a mom with teenagers, and out of one of her drawers, I unearthed plastic place mats with multiplication tables.

Food

Go to the cereal aisle of any grocery store, and you'll become mesmerized by the variety. Go to a big-box store, and you'll be impressed by the never-ending supply of granola bars. You shouldn't have the same sensation when opening one of your own kitchen cabinets. Remember the advice from chapter 6, and **let a store be a store.** Your children will be fine if they have only three cereals to choose from, and so will you. Not only will it save space in your cabinets, it will also guarantee that your food will taste fresher. Save your money—and your taste buds—and buy what you can consume reasonably quickly.

In the meantime, purge what's already packing your refrigerator and freezer. **Judge the freshness of every perishable item, and discard what's past its prime.** Dig into your freezer and make sure you know what's lurking in its farthest recesses. Especially for families with young children who go through frozen waffles and pizza by the handful, freezer storage is a necessity of life. But we get into trouble when we forget that we are not snowed in for the winter, we can make it to a grocery store if need be. **Remember, freezer items are perishable, too**, especially meats and anything with a high water content. How many times have you unearthed an expensive freezer-burned cut of meat? Unless it's vacuum-packed for the purpose of freezing, you're better off never putting meat in the freezer, because it won't taste as good once it's been frozen. It's far preferable to **purchase only the meat you can consume before the sell-by date.**

Turn your attention to nonperishables. **Consider how likely it is that each pantry item will be eaten,** such as canned goods that have seen more than one anniversary. Sure, they may be edible, but will they be sitting there unused another year from now? If so, then you're not likely to eat them and they're taking up space. Donate them to a soup kitchen or food pantry.

Finally, a word about the spice rack: Any chef will tell you that spices and herbs lose their flavor over time. But most of us who cook (and even some of us who don't) have a selection of about fifty dry spices and herbs in our cabinets, and we're understandably hesitant to get rid of any because they can be expensive to replace. So how long can you keep herbs and spices? Dry spices can last several years and maintain their potency, but if the last time you used that garam masala was ten years back, it may be time to say goodbye. Herbs lose their potency much faster. If your herbs don't smell fragrant when crushed in your palm, then they are past their prime and should be discarded. Date your spices and herbs when they're purchased, and purge them the way you would anything in your kitchen. When you have a compact selection, you'll be much more likely to find and use what you have. And remember: **Just because a spice exists, that doesn't mean you have to own it.**

Cookbooks and Recipes

A client of mine had shelves and shelves of Asian cookbooks, all of which he insisted he used. He dug in his heels when I suggested cutting back, but I'm relentless, and eventually, I got him to admit he could live happily with far fewer. If you love your cookbooks, keep a nice selection on your living room bookshelves, but **the kitchen is the place for only the cookbooks that you use so much, the pages are stained.**

Toss all those recipe books that nursery schools circulate (you know the ones I'm talking about—where they ask all the families to contribute favorite dishes). Do you really need Sam's grandmother's noodle kugel recipe? Are you really ever going to make Play-Doh from scratch? I'll answer for you: no and no.

Purging cookbooks is the easy part. For my clients who love to cook and subscribe to cooking magazines, the real problems are the piles of clippings from newspapers, pages torn out of magazines, and even the magazines themselves, all piled up on the counter waiting for their moment in the sun. Sadly, that moment rarely comes, because the pile is so daunting and disorganized that you couldn't possibly remember what's in there or find that one recipe you might be looking for. Here are some tips for how best to pare way down:

- Pull out the recipes you want, and recycle the magazines.

- Ask yourself if any of the recipes might be available online. Recipes printed in newspapers and magazines are almost always searchable if you have a subscription. There are plenty of freely accessible food blogs and websites with a wealth of recipes to choose from. Toss the print version of anything you can obtain digitally. For more about keeping digital recipes, see steps 2 and 3.

- Go through your entire pile of torn-out recipes and decide what to keep. Unless it's a special-occasion recipe, toss anything you have kept for a year but haven't yet made.

- Get rid of all recipes that contain ingredients that your family hates; you're highly unlikely to make them.

- Remember my advice to think about the life you lead, not the one you aspire to. Do you keep pulling out recipes with special ingredients that you don't have or never make that special trip to find? Have you ever cooked one of those recipes? If not, get rid of them. Often we pull out recipes that we'd like to *eat* while not asking ourselves if we'd enjoy *cooking* them. Those are two different things.

Steps 2 and 3: Design and Organize

Let's look at the design of your kitchen storage and clarify the tools and strategies to help keep you organized in each area.

Open Storage

Open shelving in kitchens has become really popular, but I'm not a big fan. Too often it becomes a jumble that adds to visual clutter. I encourage my clients who insist on open shelving to **display only the items that look attractive**, such as coordinated sets of enameled cast-iron or copper pots or a beautiful assortment of bowls or vases. Use closed cabinet storage for everything else.

Cabinets

The vast assortment of organizers available at home stores, as well as specialty kitchen and organizing stores, can help you maximize and organize your cabinet storage. Some are designed especially for plates and bowls so you don't have to stack things deeply, risking chips and breakage. There are also shelf expanders for glasses and cups, and organizers for keeping lids and pans tidy.

Bear in mind that room can be made in cabinets when you move *out* the large items. One easy way to make space is to remove the huge pot that you only use once a year for chili. That can go in the top of a closet somewhere else in the home. The same thing goes for the standing mixer if you use it once or twice a year for cookies.

One last note about the things we tend to store in cabinets: I encourage my clients to take better advantage of the big, lovely bowls and pitchers that they so rarely use. Turn that gorgeous wedding gift into a fruit bowl for the kitchen counter—that's what I call beautifully designed organization.

Pantry

Anything that comes in a box can be stored directly in a cabinet, but foods that come in bags—such as grains, some pastas, flours, and sugars—create a messy jumble, especially once opened. These items should be transferred to matching labeled clear storage containers, which has the added benefit of keeping things safe from insects. When storing pasta this way, buy only one brand of any particular shape and type to ensure that you're not mixing pastas with different cooking times (and then you can label the container accordingly). **Square storage containers are best for maximizing space, and they can also be stacked.** Just remember that you should always consume everything in the storage container before restocking it—for example, don't pour new flour on top of old flour.

As with everything in the house, store your pantry items where you use them, and store like with like. **Think about your food not just in terms of what it is but also what it's used for and when.** If you keep your coffeepot in one corner of the kitchen counter, then store coffee, tea, sweeteners, and filters in a cabinet right above—if you have the room, the mugs could go there as well. Maybe that's also the cabinet where you store your vitamins for the morning.

You'll want to **store pantry items such as beans, rice, pasta, canned broth, and tomatoes, etc., in one section of staples.** Shelf expanders are great for maximizing space for canned goods. **Store your spices in the same cabinet as your flours, cocoa, sugars, and salts.** For families in which the kids do a lot of baking, I recommend keeping a labeled box that can contain all the sprinkles and decorating items—including the cookie cutters you purged in step 1—so it's always handy and organized for the next baking project. Ideally, store all baking-related items in a cabinet near or directly above where you tend to do your mixing.

Finally, **if you want your children to start getting their own snacks, then it makes sense to store all those snack-related items in a single cabinet that they can reach.** That might be where you put the cereal, if your children are big cereal eaters. I've been in lots of homes where the cereal is stored way up high where children can't reach it, which doesn't help when you're trying to encourage independence.

Refrigerator and Freezer

It will come as no surprise to you that I'm a little bit of a maniac when it comes to my fridge. First of all, I don't have anything stuck to the front of it—no pictures or random notes attached with magnets. **The refrigerator door is not the spot for creative expression—it's an appliance.** The only thing I allow my clients to put on their refrigerator door is a master calendar (for more on this concept, see chapter 10).

Inside my refrigerator, the milk cartons are lined up at perfect right angles. Everything is evenly spaced, and I know where everything is. One time a few of my friends decided that it would be hilarious to "reorganize" my refrigerator for me. I didn't freak out when I opened the fridge door to find the contents completely shuffled, but I want you to know that I don't let those friends into my kitchen unsupervised anymore.

In terms of how to store what you have, **think of your refrigerator and freezer the same way you would your pantry, and store like with like.** Designate a place for everything. I always line up my milk on the widest shelf, with the unopened containers in the back. I keep the perishable pasta sauces and dinner items on a different shelf. The drawers in the fridge can be your guide for organizing the rest. I don't freeze a lot, so I have three types of items, each kept in its own compartment: 1) breakfast food, such as bagels and waffles;

2) ice cream; and 3) dinner foods, such as vegetables, leftovers, and frozen meals.

As in the kitchen cabinets, the most space-efficient storage containers for the fridge and freezer are square and stackable. You can use plastic if you prefer it; however, plastic isn't microwave-safe, so if you want to reheat something, you have to transfer it to a different dish. I love glass storage containers that can go from fridge to freezer to microwave. Some can even go into the oven. Purchase only one type of storage, for easier stacking and easier matching of tops to bottoms.

Cookbook and Recipe Storage

The tightly edited selection of books that you wish to keep in the kitchen should go on an open shelf, if you have one, or they can be lined up in a kitchen cabinet, which has the added benefit of keeping them clean. Either way, **books should *not* be kept on the kitchen counter.** You want to keep that surface area clear.

If you're attached to your purged selection of recipes pulled out of newspapers and magazines, then **get an accordion file or a standing file with folders and organize your recipes by category**: weeknight dinners, desserts, dinner party menus, etc.

Finally, there are several excellent recipe apps that can free you from the paper pile-up. As a result, in many kitchens, that splattered pile of clippings can be replaced by your smartphone or tablet. Keep a digital folder of bookmarked recipes to use in the kitchen, and refer to them when you're in the grocery store contemplating what to make for dinner. **Go digital in the kitchen as much as possible.**

Step 4: Maintain

The kitchen undergoes a lot of wear and tear on a daily basis, so it's especially important to maintain your new organization practices—otherwise, things could easily fall into disarray again. The key to long-term maintenance is to simplify. Cut extra steps and complications wherever you can, prepare ahead of time, and establish some clear-cut routines for you and everyone else in the family. Here are some tips, as well as typical problem areas and long-term solutions:

1. *Keep a grocery list.* Every member of the family should use it, and it should be kept in a prominent location—posted on the refrigerator, mounted on a wall, or left on a corner of one counter, if you have the space. I have my family trained: If an item is on the grocery list, it gets purchased—within reason, of course. But if they run out of something that they didn't put on the grocery list, then they're not allowed to come complaining to Mom. As I mentioned in chapter 6, it's good to keep one central list for all the household items, since so much of the shopping gets done at the same stores. You get extra points if you can keep a copy of this list on your smartphone, where it's always handy.

2. *Control purchases.* Buy only the perishable items that you can consume prior to a) their expiration date; and b) your next shopping trip. Buy only nonperishables that you will consume in the next three months.

3. *Plan dinners once a week.* If you make one big grocery trip a week, set aside time beforehand to look at your family's calendar and plan meals. If you keep bookmarked recipes or an accordion file system, this is a great time to flip through that folder of family dinners and decide what you might like to make. Now look in your pantry to see what ingredients you have and add what you need to your grocery list.

4. *Remember, you're not running a restaurant.* It's hard enough coping with the picky eaters in your own family, but trying to

cater to other people's allergies and restrictions when you're entertaining can get impossible. A friend of mine was beside herself when she had six people over for dinner and half of the guests were low-carb and the other half were vegetarian. Cooking a satisfying meal for vegetarians when pasta, starch, and most beans and grains were out of the question was no easy feat. I have dear relatives who will drive themselves crazy accommodating everyone's tastes by making five different main courses. *Just say no.* Putting aside food allergies that must be accommodated, it's simply polite to eat what you're served or whatever dishes your dietary restrictions allow you. If you're hosting and requirements get too complicated for your stress level, then it's perfectly fine to order in or suggest meeting at a restaurant.

5. *Stick with what you do well.* Whether or not you're a natural entertainer, I guarantee that you will have more fun entertaining if you have a few menus that you do well and that you repeat over and over. You can even serve the dishes on the same platters, so you can get the whole thing down to a science. I'm a pro at Sunday brunch. I have one thing I make from scratch, other things I purchase, and I always serve everything the same way. It's the typical lox and bagels, but here's how I make it special for my guests while being easy and stress-free for me:

   - I have the bagel store preslice the bagels, and I arrange them on a long rectangular platter.
   - I put the lox on a pretty plate with wedges of lemon as garnish and decoration.
   - I put whitefish and tuna salad in mounds on a platter.
   - On another platter, I place mounds of three different kinds of cream cheese (plain, tofu, and scallion).

- Into each mound of salad or cream cheese, I put a label wrapped like a flag around a toothpick so my guests know exactly what each item is.
- I have a three-tiered platter for sweets—one level is rugelach, one is minimuffins, and the third is a pie or cake.
- The night before, I make baked cinnamon French toast that gets heated right before the guests come and served in the dish it's cooked in (it's a real crowd pleaser, and if you want the recipe, go to my website, www.resourceful consultants.com).
- Finally, I place coffee cups, cream, milk, and sugar next to my coffeemaker so guests can serve themselves, and I pour orange juice into a nice pitcher. Done and done, and everyone's happy!

6. *Teach your kids to make their own lunches.* Most moms I know absolutely loathe the lunch box drill. It's another chore added to the already busy morning, and half the time the lunches come back partially eaten. So annoying. Once your children are old enough to throw a few items together, I strongly encourage you to enlist them in taking a large share of the responsibility for lunch preparation. As soon as the box is cleaned out from the current day's lunch, it can be immediately refilled with a juice box or bottled water, a napkin, and whatever nonperishable items (granola bar, bag of chips, whatever) you choose. Prepare the sandwich the night before and sock it away in the fridge alongside any other perishable items you plan to include. Even better, sandwich making could be made a part of your child's routine, just like homework or making her own bed. The side benefit is that children are much likelier to eat something they've made themselves.

The Happy Hearth

Outside of the bathroom—the room with all the mirrors in it, as previously noted—there's probably no room in the home where we judge ourselves more harshly than in the kitchen. We wish we cooked more or better, or ate healthier or less.

We can make things easier for ourselves. When we transform the kitchen into a cleaner, more orderly, inviting place, then we're bringing ourselves much closer to our goal of a healthy attitude toward cooking and eating. Our way is clearer, our food is fresher, and we can view food preparation as more of a pleasure than a chore. At a minimum, we'll be able to find the cumin when we really do need it.

9

ROOM FOR LIVING
The Family Room
and Living Room

Company is coming this evening. What's the first thing you do, other than figure out what you're feeding them? You clean the living areas of your home. And by clean, I don't mean vacuum and dust. I mean you run around and pick up piles—often newspapers and magazines, sometimes toys. The coffee table, typically the center of the room, gets swept off, and the multiple layers that were covering it get hidden somewhere else.

Even after you do that, it's not the airy, spacious room you hoped it would be. Everything feels . . . crowded. The walls are covered in pictures that look haphazard, and more pictures and decorative items sprout from the surfaces in the room. The long-term problem is that once your company leaves, those few areas you cleared off will quickly become covered again. So let's fix this problem now and forever more.

There are large homes with separate family rooms where they put all their media, and the "living room" essentially becomes a showplace that's used only when guests arrive. That's not my concern here. I want to talk about those areas of the home that you actually *live* in.

Each family has different pleasures and priorities, and our living areas speak to that loud and clear. Some families love books, some love to collect art or exotic souvenirs from their travels. And many of us have a large television as the focal point in the living area.

There's nothing wrong with any of those priorities. The problem is when any one—or several—begin to take over and crowd the space. As with every other area of the house, you need to figure out what is most important to your family to keep in that space and what you might be able to store or display elsewhere.

Do the Squint Test on your living areas. (Refer back to chapter 2 if you need to remind yourself how it works.) In your living room, you want to have the *opposite* impression from the one you have in a closet. Here in the living room, you very much want some open spaces. If, however, your living room is looking more like your closet, with every inch of wall surface covered, then it's no wonder you're feeling a little hemmed in.

It's time to go through steps 1 through 4—figure out what you can purge, then design and organize what remains. Once you've done that, maintaining is easy. Not all the steps will apply equally to every element of the room. Let's break them up into manageable pieces and tackle each concern one at a time, applying the steps where they make the most sense.

Furniture

Many of us combine homes when we get married. We also have pieces handed down to us from parents and grandparents, as well as other random items we picked up along the way. The result is that we often have more furniture than we need. I've been in a lot of homes where the living room is starting to look like a furniture store. **Furniture, just like anything else in the home, needs to be purged.** There are only so many sideboards, end tables, and chairs that a room can or should hold before it starts to look crowded.

Take a look around your living room and think about whether there are pieces that are more for show than for utility. If your room is starting to feel cramped, think about donating the showpieces or repurposing them elsewhere in the home.

Now let's **design the best space for you.** Consider the furniture you have. Is it serving you? As noted in chapter 3, in homes where space is at a premium, furniture should do double duty. The best coffee tables have drawers as well as shelves underneath. End tables should also have storage. There are ottomans with storage inside, and some with cushions that flip over into trays to provide more surface area.

End tables and coffee tables shouldn't be crowded with framed pictures and other objects. Less is more. A vase or particularly well-designed lamp will stand out far more beautifully on a side table if it's not so surrounded that you can't see its lines.

As noted in chapter 1 and elsewhere, **a few well-edited items can look lovely and intentional when corralled by an attractive tray.** A tray is also great for gathering together a few remote controls—it can be placed on a shelf under the coffee table or near where you typically sit to watch television. An attractive covered box is even better. That can sit out on top of the coffee table. For more about purging framed photographs and other decorative items, read on in this chapter.

Hands down, **the best thing for the storage-deprived home is a built-in wall unit;** these work especially well in the living room. The best built-ins are flexible, allowing movement of shelves up or down to accommodate books and display items of different sizes. A floor-to-ceiling wall unit with closed storage at the top and bottom is a fantastic option and can look really polished.

Closed storage at the top is key. Unless you have a lot of books and you want the look of a library, or you have a great collection of large pieces (vases, for example) that will make a visual impact from a relatively far distance, then open storage at the top is a waste of space. The combination of closed and open storage is most practical for families who have collections of board games or gaming system accessories that would look messy in the open. Ultimately, **the more shelves and storage you can create on one wall, the more you can free up surfaces and wall space in the rest of the room** to give yourself some much needed air and light.

For more about how to organize your books and decorative items on your wall unit and shelves, see the next two sections in this chapter.

Books

I'm not one of those organizers who wants people to get rid of all their books. I love books—I enjoy reading them, and I appreciate the warm feeling they can give a room. However, **too many books can transform a room from cozy to claustrophobic, so it's important to purge regularly.** Here's how:

- Remove all books that you don't want to display—this means self-help on anger management, the difficult child, or finding a new job. If you refer to them, move them to a less public space, such as the office or bedroom.

- Donate any books that your children have outgrown, with the exception of a *handful* of their most beloved, if you or they are attached to them.

- Donate any books that you have read and liked but didn't love. Certainly donate any books that you didn't like.

- Donate any books that you loved but couldn't imagine reading or referring to again or wishing to loan to someone else.

- Make sure nothing is so big that it emerges past the edge of the shelf. If a book is too large to fit—and assuming you love it— move it elsewhere, such as the shelf under a coffee table.

Book lovers will have strong opinions about how they want their books placed, especially if they have signed books that they want to gather in one place, or if they like to keep together all the books by one author. That's fine, but generally speaking, books should be grouped by category: reference, biographies, fiction, etc. Within categories, the books should be lined up in height order and all pulled out to the edge of the bookshelves—and no farther. You should have tall books together and small books together. If all of your tall books are together on one shelf, you can potentially fit in an additional shelf of short books.

Those are the basics of arranging books on a bookshelf or storage unit. The next task in making your shelves look good is to intersperse the books with some decorative items. Let's talk about how to do that next.

Decorative Items and Shelf Designing

Once we've purged and categorized the books—thereby clearing some room—we can get to artfully arranging the shelves.

First you should **purge the decorative items.** Sort through all your candlesticks, bowls, vases, and collections, and make sure you are keeping only things you love and that will be shown off to their best effect on a shelf. None of the items should be so large that it would extend past the edge of the shelf.

Now look at your shelves of books and aim to create some breathing room and visual interest so that no shelf is a single block of book spines. Have fun with this—arranging shelves is more art than science. **Remember that shelves look best when they're not so formal.** For instance, it can look great to forgo bookends and instead stack some books horizontally to hold things in place. Horizontal stacking works especially well for large art books. You can set a small piece of sculpture or exceptional framed photograph on top of a horizontal stack; just be sure that it's no higher than eye level (for more about framed photographs, see the next section in this chapter). You can tuck in some decorative boxes to store small items that you wouldn't want left out—such as memo pads—or household items, such as batteries, as discussed in chapter 7. And in the more open spaces, you can display a lovely vase. Let the interior decorator hiding inside of you come out.

Framed Photographs and Wall Art

I have been in many homes where the same family photo is framed in more than one room or the quality of the photos is poor. Why frame a blurry picture? When our children are in the baby stage, it can be irresistible to frame pictures of every moment, from the first bath to the first bowl of cereal. Some of those images may stand the test of time. Others need to make room for the later stages. I've been in lots of homes where the children are teenagers, but you'd think they were permanently stuck at age five, because there's no evidence that they grew past kindergarten. I've also been in homes where the families felt obligated to display framed photos given to them by other people—of other families! I have a firm policy that **you should not have to display any item that you didn't choose and frame yourself.**

Also apply an editorial eye to the framed items on your walls and the way they fill up that space. Large pieces of art should be well chosen, and you should love them. If you have a lot of small pieces of art, they can have greater visual impact when grouped together, which can allow you to create more space between groupings, giving the eye some breathing room.

If you have galleries of family photos, avoid a haphazard look by framing them all similarly, with the same or similar frames and mats of similar widths. Avoid extremely wide mats—they dwarf the images and take up more than their share of room on the wall.

Newspapers and Magazines

A comfortable living room is one where you can put your feet up on an ottoman without having to shove off a pile of newspapers first. It's also one where there is a clear place to set down a mug of coffee. Too often a backlog of old newspapers and magazines is allowed to take up permanent residence on the coffee table and other surfaces in the room. I have clients who are so addicted to their newspapers that they will hold on to the accumulation of papers that arrived during vacation. Even weeks after their return, they can't bring themselves to recycle the arts and leisure section they missed during their trip.

Reading all your newspapers and magazines on a tablet or ereader would eliminate this problem altogether. But many of us are attached to our paper publications. I have a few hard and fast rules to prevent accumulation:

- Daily publications are recycled daily.
- Weekly publications are recycled weekly.
- Monthly publications are recycled monthly.

I suspect you are sensing a pattern! Basically, **you should never have more than one issue of the same publication.** On your coffee table (or even better, the shelf underneath) you can have a tray or a neat stack of *current* publications. If you are determined to read that ten-page essay in a month-old *New Yorker,* there's a simple solution: Rip it out and put it in your handbag, or set it in a nice tray by your bedside. Then recycle the rest of the magazine.

For those who are constantly pulling out articles about vacation spots or new restaurants or your child's college search, it's best to create file folders and store them where you keep your other files, or leave them in your inbox or on your bedside table if you're actively working on those projects. Then when you've been to Spain, or eaten at that restaurant, or your child is safely off to school, you can purge the files. (For more on filing, see chapter 10.)

Wires and Cables

Unless your television and stereo have wires concealed in the walls—which is lovely and a wonderful luxury if you can afford it—then you probably have a tangle of wires and cables blooming in a clump under the console table. If you live in an older home, chances are you're stuck with fewer electrical outlets than you might like, which means the inevitable proliferation of surge protectors and extension cords traveling along the baseboards.

I wish I could give you one perfect solution, but short of closing your eyes or forking out lots of money to an electrician, there isn't one. There are some tricks that can make those wires a tiny bit less obvious, though. Most baseboards are white, so it makes sense to choose surge protectors and extension cords that are also white. At any hardware store, you can find **plastic cable staples** for attaching the wires to your baseboards if you want them to blend with the wall as much as possible. Be careful not to damage the wires by attaching them too tightly. If you want to get a little more elaborate, you can also purchase **paintable wire covers.**

Finally, for that mass of cords that trails from your electronic equipment, the best you can do is to **smooth them out, gather them together, and bundle them with a Velcro wrap or clip tie made expressly for that purpose.** I find it helpful to use a label maker to label what each cord belongs to, then attach the label to the base of the cord, right above the plug. This way you know what you're unplugging when the need arises. After all this, it still might not look like an English garden, but at least it won't look like a jungle.

Houseplants

If you have a truly green thumb, plants can be lovely in a home. The problem occurs when a) you have a brown thumb, so your plants look awful; or b) you have such a green thumb that your home is starting to look like a greenhouse. Anything beautiful will be shown off to its best effect if it's not amid a huge assortment. **Purge the plants that aren't thriving because the light's wrong or you don't know how to take care of them.** Don't feel the need to keep that no-longer-blooming hydrangea that your children gave you for Mother's Day (trust me, they've forgotten). Unless the plants are well edited, in great shape, and in quality pots, they aren't contributing to your environment.

Instead of potted plants, consider indulging in a bouquet of cut flowers on occasion and as your budget allows. A small bouquet can look especially lovely in a bathroom and can enliven any room. Just be sure to toss them once they're past their prime.

Home Sweet Home

I started this book warning what a mistake it is to compare our homes to what we see in a catalog or a magazine. Nowhere is that more tempting than in our living areas. We put a lot of weight and expectation on those spots—they're our public spaces, but they're also where we do a lot of our private living.

Here's some reassurance for you: No one feels comfortable when surrounded by clutter. *But* I guarantee you that no one would feel comfortable in a magazine ad, either. Homes are meant to be lived in, and living rooms are *definitely* mean to be lived in. The goal of this chapter—and this book—isn't to sterilize your home; it's to make space for all the wonderful experiences with which you want to fill it. So go ahead, take a load off, and pour yourself some wine—and take a moment to enjoy the fact that there's now room for your feet and your glass.

10

THE COMMAND CENTER
The Home Office

I like to think that I put my clients at ease right away when I visit them in their homes. I know they're putting a lot of trust and faith in me—after all, they're opening up all their most private spaces to me. And the area of the house that can be the *most* stressful in this way is the home office.

When I start poking my nose into my clients' files and papers, they're not anxious about all the confidential financial information I'm privy to. No, they're most often on edge because they're embarrassed that their office areas are such a mess, and they're afraid that I'm going to be horrified. I always assure my clients that no matter how bad things are, I've seen much, much worse. Honestly, I have. I've been in homes that were gradually being swallowed by paper accumulation—bills and tax forms mixed in with yellowing newspapers and every Pottery Barn catalog ever printed. Though most of us aren't that bad off, we do have those stacks of paper that give us agita every time we look at them, or the email inbox that's so jammed with stuff that we regularly miss or can't find the emails that we really need. Many of us have double-booked an engagement, or overcommitted ourselves, or been late with a bill.

Anything to do with finances, insurance forms, taxes, scheduling, and the myriad clerical items that keep a household running can be a huge source of anxiety. We think that if we're not on top of it all, then we've failed in some essential way. We judge our success as adults and caretakers for our families by how well we handle these things. But it's not surprising that this area of the house can get so out of control.

Number one, these tasks are not fun. No one *enjoys* paying bills and filing life insurance policies or juggling a family calendar that looks more complicated than a political campaign schedule.

Number two, we often don't know where to begin to get ourselves organized. We don't know what to keep and where—or how—to keep it. Maybe we don't have the right furniture, lots of households don't have the luxury of a designated spot for a desk and filing cabinets. Even those households that do have office areas aren't immune to messes.

It doesn't necessarily mean that we're inherently disorganized. Many of my clients work in offices outside the home and never miss an appointment or a deadline in their business lives. Why? Because they have filing cabinets, calendars, electronic reminders, and weekly meetings—all kinds of systems are in place for keeping them organized. The key word in that sentence is, of course, "systems."

An organized home office is a lot easier to achieve than you might think. Chances are, many of your current problems are self-created, and if you eliminate those unnecessary roadblocks, you will find your path much, much clearer. Because the office is such a big subject, we're going to break it down into parts. First we'll talk about the structure of your office; then we'll address each of the tasks you perform there.

Creating an Organized Office

When we're allocating space in the home, the office is not always a huge priority—we're typically more concerned with adequate bedrooms and living areas. The home office gets relegated to whatever space is left over, if any. When my twins were born, my home office got turned into a playroom, and I ended up taking over the pantry. If yours is little more than a spare corner, rest assured that when I refer to "home office," I don't necessarily mean a room with a door—I mean "office" in a more virtual sense. Your home office is wherever you pay the bills and do the emailing, scheduling, and clerical work of your household. That could be a room, or it could be a spot at the kitchen table.

Step 1: Purge

When my son, Matthew, was in kindergarten, he went on a playdate at a friend's house and happened to take a wrong turn into the home office. What he found there shook him to the core: stacks of papers piled floor to ceiling. He closed the door, walked into the kitchen, and said to his friend's mother, "You know, my mom's a professional organizer. She can help you with that." That's my boy.

It will come as no great shock to you that I advocate minimalism in offices. A few pictures and a bulletin board can make your desk area feel warm. But your desk shouldn't be a display area for your *Star Wars* figurine collection, and your bulletin board should be tidy and well edited, with everything at right angles. You could post a few forthcoming invitations, a class calendar, and an appealing postcard or two. When items start to overlap, you know you've got too much and it's time to purge. We'll talk about how to purge papers and documents later. For now, focus on removing anything from your desk area that doesn't absolutely belong there.

Steps 2 and 3: Design and Organize

The less space you have for a desk or computer, the more you should maximize vertical space. Use empty walls for bookshelves or wall units. A closed cabinet is great for less attractive items, and even space in the living room can be commandeered for closed storage—a laptop and some hanging files and a box of supplies can be tucked away, and there you have it: a portable home office. There are also wardrobes that double as offices, although you need to have the floor space.

No matter what size your space is, you don't need many tools to keep you organized. All that's required are:

☐ **A place to keep essential supplies** (such as paper, envelopes, pens, tape, scissors, and a stapler). This could be a box that goes on a shelf or a desktop organizing system. Space will be your guide. The important thing is that you have a central location and you know where to find the items when you need them.

☐ **A master calendar.** Whether it's print or electronic matters less than the fact that you have one calendar that contains all your family's activities (see more on the master calendar later in this chapter).

☐ **An inbox.** This can be a tray or a box, and it is for a very select group of items that you can't act on immediately, such as an invitation that requires checking with family members. It is not a catchall.

☐ **A place to put files.** If you have a designated office space, then you have your choice of filing cabinets, but even if space is tight to nonexistent, all you need is a filing box or two. Many are attractive enough to go unnoticed in a living room.

☐ **A place for bills and a checkbook.** I recommend keeping this space separate from the inbox. It could be a tray or basket or a closed box. The important thing is that you have a regular schedule for dealing with it: pay bills once a week and always on the same day of the week. My husband does ours on Sunday evenings; we're always at home then, and he can ask me questions if need be.

☐ **A paper shredder.** If you're doing a big purge of private paper clutter, then this comes in really handy. Otherwise, you can just shred by hand.

Step 4: Maintain

In the rest of this chapter, we'll establish the systems to help you maintain order in the future. Let's get philosophical for a moment and talk about the attitudes and behaviors we need for long-term maintenance. To some extent, all of the commandments outlined in chapter 1 can be applied to the office, but there are a few that I find particularly helpful, and they bear repeating:

• **Do the thing that is most distasteful to you first.** It's Commandment 1 for a reason. Nothing gets better by being put off longer—at least not when it comes to taxes, bill paying, and filing. The tax situation will become more stressful, the payments will be late and fines will be accrued, and the filing will accumulate and become more tedious. If you hate it, do it now.

- **Store things where you use them.** Commandment 6 is especially helpful in the office. Get your exercise at the gym, not walking to your filing cabinet. The closer your file drawers or box are to your desk, the more likely you are to file those papers and not stack them in a pile.

- **Routines work.** As noted, Commandment 2 works in any situation, and it's the only way to keep on track with tasks you dislike. This means that every night you should spend a little time putting all your desk items where they belong—bills with bills, inbox items in the inbox, etc. A few minutes invested on a daily basis will save a big time-consuming headache when you'd rather be doing other things.

- **Make a decision and act on it.** Commandment 10 saves *so* much time that you might have wasted on dithering. Make it your goal to touch each task only once. Read the email, then immediately reply. Get the doctor receipt and submit it for insurance. Don't pick it up, look at it, then put it back down to deal with it later (rinse, repeat).

Paper and Documents

There are two things that contribute most to paper accumulation. The first is uncertainty about what's important and how long it should be kept. The second is not keeping a strong enough rein on the amount of paper coming into the home in the first place. Let's go through the steps and address both issues.

Step 1: Purge

If your desk currently looks like a burial mound, I want you to ask yourself a question: How much of the information found on those papers can also be found online? Are you receiving printed statements that are available electronically? Bear that in mind as you purge. **If you can find it online or store it electronically, then you don't need the paper.** By all means, tell your bank and credit card companies that you don't need paper statements in the future.

So many different kinds of papers and records pass our desks and cause us stress, and as noted above, we often don't know what we should keep and how long. Here are some general guidelines to help you navigate that obstacle course. Your individual needs may vary, and you should always check with your personal financial adviser and/or accountant for more specific advice.

1. Junk receipts

You know the ones I mean: the receipts you get from Starbucks for a cup of coffee; for the newspaper and bottle of water you purchased at the airport; for that salad you bought for lunch. These receipts are all trash. Shred them or toss them or don't take them in the first place. Remember, even the IRS doesn't want receipts for items under twenty-five dollars, and if you pay with a credit or bank card, then you already have an electronic record of those purchases.

2. ATM receipts

Are you still requesting the receipt every time you use the ATM? Stop that! Remember, there is no bank record that you can't get online. If you do have an accumulation of ATM receipts, shred them.

3. Non-tax-deductible, non-insurance-related receipts

If you ordered something online, there is no reason to keep the receipt that comes with the shipment—your receipt is electronic and can be kept in a file marked "receipts" in your email inbox, or it can be retrieved from the retailer's website. If you purchased the item in a physical store, then hold on to the receipt until you've worn the item, used it, or otherwise made sure it works and suits your needs. If the item is under warranty, keep the receipt stapled to the warranty and file it (more on filing systems when we get to steps 2 and 3).

4. Big-ticket items and insurance-related receipts

It's wise to keep receipts for anything in your home that could be claimed in an insurance policy in case of theft or damage. Keep these in your insurance file.

5. Tax-deductible receipts

Assuming you filed your taxes annually and you haven't committed fraud, the IRS has three years in which to decide to audit your return for any innocent human error. Any paper receipts older than three years (that don't fall into the other categories here) can be shredded.

6. Tax returns

Seven years. Interesting: the same allotment of bad luck you get if you break a mirror.

7. Bank statements

These are all available online. As noted above, opt out of printed statements, if possible.

8. Retirement accounts and other investments

Keep quarterly statements until you receive the annual, then shred all quarterly statements. Keep annual statements.

9. Mortgage and house purchase receipts

Keep everything until you sell, then follow tax return guidelines.

10. Loan statements

Keep loan agreements until the loan is paid off, but any statements that can be found online should be left that way.

11. Medical records

Keep all records for ongoing medical issues (more on how to file these below). Keep records of recent and/or significant vaccinations and test results, but only the most recent set. You don't need the records of your cholesterol count or your normal mammogram for the last ten years; just your most recent results will do.

12. Insurance policies

You need only your most recent policies; all old policies can be tossed.

13. Last will and testament

Always keep a copy of your most recent will.

As you continue purging your desk, get rid of anything that you don't need or that you are not acting upon (or never acted upon and now its usefulness is void, such as coupons and special offers, cultural event season calendars, etc.). Once you've finished shredding and recycling, move on to the paper that you do have to keep.

Step 2: Design

As I've mentioned elsewhere, one of the biggest barriers between most people and their desire to get organized is that they're convinced that a system has to be complicated in order to work. The problem isn't that they don't have enough files; it's that they have too many. As a result, filing becomes such an onerous task that it doesn't get done. The best filing system is easy and logical and doesn't break everything down into tiny categories. Here are the basic supplies you need:

☐ **Label maker.** I've recommended this elsewhere, and if you haven't treated yourself to one yet, you will be amazed at how much better your files will look if you use one for labeling your folders and hanging tabs.

☐ **Hanging file folders and tabs.** Whatever color you choose is fine as long as it's all the same. This is key to eliminating visual noise and clutter.

☐ **Single-tab folders.** Instead of having three- or five-tab folders, I like the single-tab folders for two reasons. First, I hate when a file label is too long for the tab. Second, having three tabs creates more visual noise. All your folders should match in color.

Generally speaking, in your filing cabinet or box, every single-tab folder will have its own hanging folder—this way, if you retrieve a folder, you always know where to return it (the empty hanging folder is like the empty hanger in your closet that tells you where your sweater goes). The hanging folders should be grouped by category, and the first hanging folder in each category will have a tab with the name of that larger category.

Step 3: Organize

Every person or family will have their own must-have files that apply specifically to their lives and histories. But generally speaking, there are a few standard categories that most if not all of us have. I'm going to walk you through how to deal with each, but no matter what you're filing, this system can apply. Wherever possible, think big, not small. Don't have one folder marked AUTO INSURANCE and another marked AUTO REGISTRATION and another marked LICENSE RENEWAL. Just have one AUTO file. The same goes for CHILDREN'S ACTIVITIES—there's no reason to break them down into subcategories (ballet, soccer, etc.).

1. Medical

The first hanging folder in any category is given a tab and labeled with the category name, in this case, MEDICAL. Inside this hanging folder is a single-tab file folder labeled INSURANCE AND RECEIPTS. All your family members' claims and receipts go in there (in chronological order, with the most recent at the front), since presumably, you all have the same insurance plan. If you don't, and you have different claims for each plan, you may want to create separate folders, which would each have a hanging folder and would immediately follow the general MEDICAL hanging folder.

In my family, there are four folders that follow the general MEDICAL file, one for each of my family member's medical records. These hanging folders don't have tabs, because they don't need them; they all fall under the larger category of MEDICAL. Each hanging folder contains a single-tab file folder labeled with the person's name (*Barbara Medical*, and so on). In the medical file for each family member, put any results from mammograms, colonoscopies, prescriptions for contact lenses or glasses, immunization records, etc.

If your doctors don't submit insurance claims for you or they're out-of-network, then you might want to keep a folder of blank claim forms for each member of the family, with the nonvariable details filled in (name, social security number, birth date, etc.) When you receive a medical bill, you can staple it to the form (on which you've written "see attached" under treatment description) and mail it in to the insurance company. I do this for my family, and it saves so much time and tedium.

KEEPING TRACK OF INSURANCE CLAIMS

Whatever your opinion of insurance companies, it's a universally accepted truth that they can be monumentally impenetrable bureaucracies. Especially for individuals with chronic medical conditions, it can begin to feel like a full-time job just to follow up on claims, reapply when claims are lost, and continually provide the additional bits of information that insurance companies always seem to need before processing your claim. Assuming that you have taken my advice to do what you hate first and you have promptly submitted your insurance claims, then keep a spreadsheet that lists the date of the doctor visit, the doctor's name, the date the claim was submitted, the amount applied to the deductible, and the amount reimbursed to you. You can create a column where you note the date that you resubmitted or sent in additional information. With this system, you'll be able to see whether the deductible has been met and whether a claim you submitted hasn't been paid. You can call to follow up (and you'll be all the more prepared to resubmit if need be).

2. Academic

Each member of your family who attends school should have an ACADEMIC file. For children, it will contain every progress report and report card and standardized test result. If there are additional reports for speech therapy, occupational therapy, etc., they go in your child's academic file chronologically, with the most recent in the front. Include in the academic file any awards or honors that may be relevant to a college application. At regular intervals, or whenever your child's file becomes full, start another single-tab folder labeled with the grades it will encompass. Generally speaking, you can purge all files as your child moves on to the next stage. Once your child gets into high school, purge the earlier grades. When your child gets to college, it's up to him or her what to keep, and you can hand that whole file over.

3. Auto

In your AUTO file, include all of the information for every car you own. Clip together the papers related to each automobile within the file, but keep them in one place. That includes a copy of the auto insurance certificate (original goes in the car), ownership documents, maintenance documents, E-ZPass documents, and garage documents.

4. Home

Instead of having separate mortgage and insurance files, have just one larger category marked HOME. In the main file, you might include all mortgage documents and closing statements, as well as your homeowners' insurance. In a subfolder marked MAINTENANCE, include a list of maintenance contacts (plumber, electrician, etc.) as well as records of repairs. Another subfolder would be WARRANTIES AND MANUALS. The receipt for the refrigerator, for example, would be stapled to the warranty, then tucked into the manual. If you find that your warranty and manual files are getting too bulky, you can transfer them to a labeled plastic container and store them in a closet. Regularly weed through manuals for items you no longer own.

5. Travel

Just one file is sufficient. Inside, you should keep everything related to travel. Clip together the etickets and itineraries for your next trip, and include a spreadsheet of any frequent-flier numbers. Some people like to keep clippings related to future travel and business cards for hotels and restaurants they enjoyed in the past. It has been my experience that by the time you're ready to take that trip, the information is out of date.

6. Important Documents

In any home filing system, it is most important to know where your important documents are kept. These include:

- ☐ passports
- ☐ birth certificates
- ☐ marriage licenses
- ☐ social security cards
- ☐ health-care proxies
- ☐ living wills
- ☐ last will and testament and trust documents
- ☐ a scan of every card (front and back) that you carry in your wallet, in case of loss or theft (you can also keep it on your computer hard drive)

Keep originals of your passports in one file, but all other items can be photocopies and kept in a single file folder. Store the originals as well as photocopies of your passports in a separate place—a safe-deposit box or some other location safe from fire and theft.

7. Financial Documents

Within the FINANCIAL category, you'll have one file for current, non-tax-deductible purchase receipts (that haven't already been filed under one of the previously outlined categories). You will want to purge it regularly.

Next you should have separate file folders for your bank and credit card statements (if you keep them on paper, but preferably you won't!). Keep folders for your retirement and investment statements. See step 1 for what to keep and for how long.

8. Tax Files

These may be the fattest in the drawer because you have to keep so many of them—seven years of filings and three years of tax-related statements and receipts can start to stack up. One option is to keep a separate file box on the upper shelf of a closet or in an under-bed container for prior-year tax documents. For the current year, you will have a folder for tax-deductible receipts; a folder for any end-of-year earnings statements and W-2s; and a folder for your most recently filed tax return.

I know, filing sounds like too much fun, right? You can't wait to buy that box of hanging folders and get started. Whether you are agreeing with me or rolling your eyes, I promise: You'll feel better when it's done.

Step 4: Maintain

Purging old files and a messy desk can be a massive job, so make sure you don't have to go through that pain and suffering again. Here's how you can radically decrease your paper accumulation going forward (and help the environment as well):

- **Consolidate your credit card accounts and bank accounts.** The more accounts you have, the more accounts you have to monitor.
- **Cancel accounts you no longer use.** Extra paperwork from unused accounts creates unnecessary clutter.
- **Avoid the temptation of new credit cards and the annoyance of insurance offers** by using OptOutPrescreen .com or by calling 1-888-567-8688 (1-888-5-OPT-OUT). You can opt out each member of your family for five years or forever!
- **Keep junk mail to a minimum** by using the Direct Marketing Association's online registry (https://www.dmachoice.org/ dma/member/regist.action). The DMA represents a wide range of legitimate businesses that use telephone, mail, and

the Internet to sell products; chances are, a large amount of
your junk mail is coming from member firms.

- **Reduce unwanted catalogs** by contacting the mail-order
  companies directly (the best method) or use a free service
  (http://www.catalogchoice.org/), which will send opt-out
  requests on your behalf.
- **Use automatic transactions** whenever possible. Pay bills
  online and have your employer use direct deposit for your
  paychecks.

Digital Decluttering

A messy computer doesn't assault the eye the way a messy desk does,
but it can get in the way of an organized life just as much—maybe
even more so, because we rely on it for so many tasks. Let's streamline
this incredibly important tool.

Digital Filing

The nice thing about a computer is that it's so easy to make files.
There's no reason not to, and it's so much better than having a jumble
of documents and files to sort through on your desktop. It's also easy
to trash documents when you're done with them. The lovely thing
about that little trash can in the corner of your computer is that, God
forbid, you make a mistake and delete something you need, you can
always find it again—although I would suggest that you empty that
trash can now and then if memory space is an issue.

View your computer (both your hard drive and your email program) the same way you do your filing cabinets. In your documents, you might have folders marked ACADEMIC, where you would put any school-related material, and so on. In your email account, you might have folders for online orders and various types of correspondence (for more on emailing, see the next section in this chapter). The wonderful thing about the computer is that it gives you such a lovely, compact place to file all those financial statements. All you have to do is convert your electronic statement to a PDF and then save it to your hard drive. Create a folder called BANK STATEMENTS, and you can instantly refer to any purchase you made, whenever. The same thing goes for credit card statements.

Bookmarks

Apply the same filing techniques to your Internet browser's bookmarks. Create folders for shopping, news, school-related websites and resources, recipes, etc. You can also create a folder for something current that you're researching (such as vacation home rental links). Once you've taken that trip, you can delete the bookmark. Weed your bookmarks regularly. I've had clients with hundreds and hundreds of unsorted bookmarks, and they've been amazed by how much more pleasurable it is to click on a folder that contains all their *favorite* sports blogs. The same thing goes for online merchants—if you don't shop at a store, then why have the bookmark?

Passwords and Log-in Names

Keeping track of these can be a chore, especially since you have to remember so many—those for online retailers, email, movie streaming services, you name it. Since many sites have different rules for log-in names and passwords, the exclamation point you use on one site may not be acceptable on another. Plus, some sites use your email address as a log-in, whereas others might use your name or some version of it. In addition, it's not considered wise, for security reasons, to use the same password on multiple accounts.

In the past, I kept all my log ins and passwords in a file with my important documents, as well as stored in a file on my password-protected hard drive. Then I discovered a far better solution to all this madness: **Get yourself an app.** There are numerous apps available across platforms, and they work brilliantly. The benefit is that you need to remember only one password: the one to get into the app. It keeps track of everything else. There are some that will even keep track of you credit card information. I love it!

Making the Most of Technology

Finally, a word about the pros and cons of relying on technology to organize our lives. If you're a technology wiz, you can ignore this part, but for the rest of us, technology can cause incredible amounts of stress and confusion. Just recently, my smartphone went on strike, and I thought my head would explode. My calendars weren't syncing, I was missing appointments (for shame!), and I genuinely did not feel like myself until I called an expert to help me fix the situation. We rely on our computers, phones, and tablets to a possibly absurd degree, so when something goes wrong with them, we panic.

My best advice is to keep it simple. I'm still not really sure what a "cloud" is, but I know that it can help me restore my contacts if something happens to my computer or smartphone. I don't care whose cloud you use, but definitely take advantage of the technology, as well as the opportunity it offers to keep your calendars in sync (more on the almighty calendar below). Have an external hard drive for your computer, and use a program to back up to it regularly. Sync your Facebook and Twitter accounts so that when you update one, the content automatically uploads onto the other. Load all of your music onto iTunes (and by all means, take that as an opportunity to purge your CD collection) so you can put together the perfect dinner-party playlist—you'll feel like such a star! The point is, technology should help you, not create more anxiety. Be strong!

Organized Emailing

Most of us spend a large percentage of our time on the computer either writing or responding to emails. Email is a huge source of clutter (and time-wasting) in our lives. Here are my rules for more orderly emailing:

- **Consolidate your accounts.** If possible, have all of your personal email accounts come into the same program.

- **Answer your emails daily, and open each only once.** In your personal life, you can get away with checking email once a day—first thing in the morning or at the end of the day, whatever works for you. In truth, if you have a smartphone, you're likely checking email all day. Either way, the key to staying on top of correspondence is to make a decision and respond. Then there are only three options once you've responded: Delete the email, put it in an email folder, or print it and put it in a paper folder.

- **Don't sign up for newsletters, instant updates, and promotional emails** that you don't want. Be highly selective. It may seem easy to delete them, but they can accumulate and tend to bury the important emails that you do need to read.

- **Use appropriate and meaningful subject lines.** They make it easier to find emails and sort by subjects. They also tell you the main point of an email at a glance. When you continue responding to an email chain, be sure to change the subject line if it no longer applies (that is, if the email chain started out being about a home repair referral and ended up being about a nursery school recommendation).

- **Don't save emails as a visual reminder to take action.** Use a to-do list for that, or create a folder marked TO DO. Having too many emails on your computer is visually chaotic and can have the opposite effect of keeping you on track. Your goal is to have empty space at the bottom of your email screen each day.

I'm just one persnickety person, so I decided to ask two certifiable email experts how to deal with some of the trickiest (often self-created and self-replicating) problems that we all encounter with email. David Shipley and Will Schwalbe wrote an incredibly helpful book called *Send: Why People Email so Badly and How to Do It Better.* Here are a few of my favorite pieces of their advice:

1. **Don't open emails until you have time to deal with them.**
   When you do, answer every one in two minutes or less, then take one of three actions with all the others: archive, delete, or move to a single follow-up folder.
2. **Be brief** when writing emails, and put the most important thing right at the top.
3. **But not too brief!** Don't forget to be cordial.
4. **Avoid hitting "reply all."** But once a Reply All festival gets started, don't jump in to chastise the culprits—it just makes things worse.
5. **You can email a thank-you.** And you can email a thank-you for an emailed thank-you. But you can't email a thank-you for an emailed thank-you to an email thank-you.

Words to live by!

Storing Images

The home office tends to be the place where we deal with our photos. Best-case scenario, the vast majority of images are saved to the computer, but I've also been in homes where there's a boxful of photos and a half-finished album collecting dust because the person responsible—Mom—ran out of steam somewhere along the way. It's no wonder, photo albums can be tedious work. We start out gung ho when our children are babies, and then we lose momentum.

Maybe you started doing albums before everything went digital. Now that all your photos are on the computer, it might be unrealistic to expect yourself to keep up with printed photo albums as well. As I've noted elsewhere, why keep something around that makes you feel bad?

First things first: **Purge whatever images that you already printed.** It may seem like a huge job, but there are just three things to do:

1. **Decide which ones are so great that you want to frame them.** Purchase frames for those images. Give yourself a deadline to complete the task; don't use it as an excuse to make another stack that never gets dealt with.

2. **Look at the remaining pictures and identify which images you like so much that you want to keep them in your album.** If those images exist digitally, consider keeping them that way—toss the print versions and organize the digital copies in albums on your computer (for more on how to do that, read on). If you don't have digital copies, then get yourself a photo album with ready-made slots and slap these photos into it. Done and done.

3. **Finally, gather together the images that don't merit framing or keeping in an album.** Now toss them. Yes, you read that right: Get rid of them.

If your primary problem is that you have years of photos on your computer and they're not organized by date, event, etc., then yes, that can be a huge job. My best advice is to set aside time as you would for any organizing task—a few hours a week–and pretty soon you'll make progress weeding and categorizing them into digital albums. Don't make yourself crazy. **If the best you can do is to sort them by year, that's better than nothing.** The important thing is that you start fresh now—that way, the problem will never get any worse, which is some consolation (right?).

For all new images, purge as you take them. Review pictures on your digital camera and delete the unfocused or unflattering images. If you took several pictures of the same subject/angle/background, pick the best one. Do that again when you download the images onto your computer (and by all means do this promptly). Finally, **don't print a single picture unless you have a frame or an album ready and waiting to be filled.** You can keep a digital backup on your computer.

When you download pictures to your computer, there are three basic steps to organizing them:

1. **Create an album** of the event. Title each album with the name of the event and the date, such as "Sara's First Birthday Party, May 2, 2012."
2. **Drag/transfer** all of the pictures into the album.
3. **Edit the pictures.** Crop out "background noise" and eliminate redeye. You can also erase your under-eye circles and brighten the colors if you like to play around with that stuff.

After you've done this, I highly recommend that you **create a "best of" folder for each family member.** You can also have "Best of Family" and "Best of Extended Family" folders. Into these folders would go your very favorite images. That will save you huge amounts of time when you want to put together a collage for your spouse's next big birthday, your parents' fiftieth wedding anniversary, or your daughter's bat mitzvah.

Finally. I don't mean to minimize the appeal of a physical photo album. There is something lovely about sitting down by yourself or with your family and flipping through images that bring back fond memories or laughter at what we were wearing. But don't let that task become an albatross around your neck. Instead, **take advantage of one of the fantastic online photo book services that can turn your digital images into a bound book.** You can make them for yourself, and they can be great presents for grandparents or thank-you gifts for that lovely week that you spent with friends.

Mail Sorting, Beyond the Basics

We talked in chapters 1 and 2 about dealing with mail at the door (recycling catalogs, etc.). There's more to mail than keeping the bills and recycling the junk. Rule number one is to **open mail with your checkbook, credit card, and calendar ready to go.** If you want to move up to the advanced level, I can't tell you how much time I have saved by memorizing the credit card number that I use the most.

As noted, when you open your mail, follow Commandment 10— **make a decision and act on it.** You want to touch each piece of paper just once, if possible. Bills can be put in your bill-paying tray or box for that once-a-week chore. Discard all the ads and special offers that get stuck in with bills, and discard the mailing envelope; if you pay online, you can discard everything but the bill or statement.

For everything else, **if you can deal with it now, why not?** If you know you're accepting or rejecting an invitation, then do that and make a note of it in your calendar. Keep the invite only if you need the information it contains. If you receive a reminder to schedule a dental appointment, put that on your to-do list or call right away; don't add the postcard to your stack of paper.

What about all that in-between correspondence (a birthday card with no special message, a thank-you note that isn't particularly sentimental)? Indulge in a smile that the sender was thoughtful, then toss it. You do not have to keep a greeting-card writer's sentiments for all of eternity. You also don't have to keep other people's holiday cards with family pictures. Remember, it's hard enough staying on top of pictures of your own children, much less other people's.

I admit that there will be some correspondence that you can't discard or respond to immediately. It goes in your inbox. An example would be an invitation to a party for which you need to ask your spouse or children if they want to attend. Then, make it a routine to **go**

through your inbox once a week, the same way you do your bills. I go through my inbox on Sunday evenings, when my husband is doing our bill paying. I also take some time to look over the master calendar for the coming week, remind myself of what our commitments are, and update my to-do list.

Scheduling

This is a massive issue for moms, because we tend to be the family cruise director—making the plans with friends and family, booking the activities and doctor appointments. There is one tool that can handle the onslaught: the master calendar. We're going to discuss how that works, then clarify how to deal with some of the typical scheduling problems we all encounter.

The Master Calendar

Perhaps one of the following scenarios sounds frighteningly familiar:

1. Your spouse says, "I didn't realize your parents were coming this weekend. I have clients in from out of town that we're taking out."
2. You have the sinking feeling that you agreed to attend a birthday party the same weekend as the big soccer tournament.
3. Your child tells you at nine on Sunday night that there's a *big* project due the following day and he hasn't even started.

4. Fifteen minutes before a work presentation, your child calls wondering why you haven't picked her up yet.

Are you sweating and experiencing heart palpitations? I know I am. These are the anxiety dreams of modern life. The only way to inoculate yourself from the terror is to embrace the concept of a master calendar. Worship it. Live by it.

It doesn't matter so much to me whether you love your old-fashioned Filofax or you're attached at the hip to your BlackBerry or iPhone. What matters is that you have one master calendar and you refer to it constantly. Some families like to have a big calendar on the refrigerator or some public place. I prefer that the master calendar be portable, so you always have it with you (when you go to the dentist and need to schedule the next appointment, or when your spouse calls you at work and asks if you're free the third weekend in September). If you keep the calendar electronically, you can sync it across devices. Again, **no matter what kind of calendar you choose, the important thing is that it holds everything**—doctor appointments, weekend plans, school activities, sports practices . . . Everything.

One practice I follow religiously is to schedule my next appointment right as I'm leaving my current appointment. If you like to have lunch with a friend once a month but it ends up being once every six months because of busy schedules, then why not schedule your next lunch date while you're waiting for your check to arrive? You know how often you need to get your hair done, so go ahead and schedule the next appointment on your way out. You can do this for dental appointments and orthodonture as well—any appointments that occur more often than once a year. For every member of my family, I **schedule annual doctor appointments around birthdays.** Then there's no need to check when your last gynecological appointment was or when your child had his last annual.

If there are two adults in the household, both members should be contributing items to the master calendar and checking with each other before adding anything major to it (this is when an electronically synced calendar can be particularly handy). Checking with each other is key. If you do all of the shepherding to appointments, then you don't need to compare notes about the dental appointment you scheduled for your son. But **anything that would eat into family time or require the presence of the other spouse must be shared, preferably in advance.** If one of you has a work dinner, then you should not only mark it in the calendar but also check with each other first to be sure there won't be a child-care issue. Never, ever make weekend plans without confirming with the spouse first. (Bonus points: You'll save money by not having to hire divorce lawyers!)

As your children get older, consult with them about scheduling matters as well. Adolescents are making their own plans, and no matter how you may have trained them, they won't always be sharing their commitments with you or adding them to the master calendar. A friend of mine gave me the excellent advice to have a **once-a-week family meeting** to discuss what's happening in the coming week. In the spirit of full disclosure, I will admit that while I would love to do this in my own family, not everyone else is so enthused. So we don't do it, but I wish we did! I know for a fact that it works for families with very young children as well as teenagers. The idea is that everyone contributes, and it's an opportunity to share logistics as well as feelings. One person can write down what was discussed (each person's high and low points of the previous week, for instance), and it can become a wonderful family journal. It shouldn't be onerous or involved; just a few lines per meeting is fine. You can keep a spiral notebook or add pages to a hanging file, the most recent to the front.

Learning to Say No

I once had a client, Alison, whose first call to me was one of utter panic and desperation. She had missed yet another birthday party of a close friend's child, and the friend had insisted that Alison needed to get her act together. Basically, the friend staged a one-woman intervention. When I stepped in to help Alison, I realized that the problem wasn't so much that she was disorganized; it was that she said yes to every invitation or request for her time.

My first task with the overscheduled moms I work with is to teach them how to say no. Many of them don't realize that it's entirely valid to ask themselves if they *want* to attend a particular event; if their family will enjoy it; if their presence will be missed; and if it's genuinely a worthwhile obligation. Those are essential barometers to apply to any proposed obligation. You should also calculate not just the time you will spend on the activity itself but also the travel to and from, the possible need for child care, and any other responsibilities you might be juggling. The first rule of social engagements is: **Think before you answer.** If the answer is no, then the second rule is: **Say no, not why.**

I'll give you an example of the two rules in practice. Recently, my family was invited to brunch at the home of a work colleague. It was a kind invitation, but it was Sunday afternoon, which is precious family time—especially when you have children who play sports and two parents who work. I knew that we wouldn't know anyone else at the brunch, and that my children would have no friends there. I concluded that our answer to the invitation should be no. We didn't have a conflict, so I couldn't say we were busy. I just said, "Thanks so much for the invitation, we're so sorry we can't attend, and it sounds like a wonderful time." No explanation. *"We can't"*—that's it.

Saying no takes practice. I have clients who waste immeasurable mental energy thinking about what to say. They look at the invitation and move it from pile to pile, never responding. Or they open the Evite again and again, never committing either way. The key, once again, is to say no, not why.

If you have a direct conflict, you could tell your friend that your son's soccer game is at the same time as her child's birthday party. Just bear in mind that she might think her son's birthday party is way more important than your child's soccer game. If you tell your friends that you can't come to a dinner party because you can't get a babysitter, they may be annoyed that they manage to get child care for their children and why can't you? What seems like a perfectly good excuse to you may seem like a cop-out to someone else. It's better not to give an excuse at all.

And of course never, ever, ever lie. If you tell a lie, then you have to maintain the lie, and eventually, you will get caught. Maybe you say you can't go to the party because it's your niece's birthday the same day. Then your friend runs into your niece and says happy birthday, and your niece says it's not her birthday. Oops.

Sticky Social Situations

What if the request for your time comes from a good cause, such as your child's school? Go to any PTA meeting and look around at who is doing most of the volunteering. Are you nodding knowingly right now? You should be.

Moms are constantly getting recruited for chaperoning, fundraising, bake sales, event setup, you name it—even if we are too busy, we have a hard time saying no. We worry that not helping out might make us bad mothers or that we'll be judged by the moms who are volunteering, and let's face it, we probably are.

My best advice with volunteering is to play to your strengths and enthusiasms. If you love to bake but hate to ask for money, then make cookies for the bake sale and don't join the fund-raising committee. If you're a working parent of a young child, maybe you'd most like to spend your volunteering time on in-class activities or field-trip chaperoning, not on things that take you away from time with your child. Finally, remember that when you are invited to volunteer, the same rules of engagement apply: Think before you answer, and if the answer is no, don't explain. "I'm sorry, I can't, and I wish you well because it's such a worthwhile cause" is a perfectly fine response. If you genuinely would like to be of help in the future, then you can say, "I can't now, but please ask again." If you say that, then you must mean it, because you *will* be asked again.

Sometimes, I will admit, it's not so easy for me to beg off, no matter how much I may want to. There are some social engagements you can't avoid, such as a boss's holiday cocktail party. At those times I give my clients a phrase to keep in mind: **Leave the party before the party leaves you.** It's all about maximizing your face time with the host—you arrive early, when there aren't so many people there (and what host doesn't appreciate that?), you spend some quality time chatting, and then you get while the getting's good.

Or maybe it's not an event you can't avoid, it's a person. There are those relentless people to whom it's hard to say no. Somehow they always manage to corner you, and they have such a forceful way that you find yourself stuttering. Email was invented for these situations— or at least that's my version of the history of email. All you have to do face-to-face is say, "Thanks so much, I just need to check with my calendar/husband/children/mother/parole officer, and I'll get right back to you." You know what to say in your follow-up email, right? No, not why.

You Can't Do It All

When we're looking at the master calendar or sitting down at the computer to answer email or pay bills, life can start to feel . . . overwhelming. So many things *must* get done, and so many other things *should* get done. As a result, the things that we'd love to do can get shoved way down to the bottom of the to-do list.

If there is one message you should take away from this chapter, it's that you can't do it all. The advice here will help you with those things that *must* get done—paying the bills and staying on top of the doctor appointments, for example. In the future, you'll hopefully find those must-do things a little easier and less time-consuming. Then you'll start to look at your list of should-dos with a fresh eye—you'll begin to say no a bit more often and yes a bit more judiciously. And then you can finally carve out some more time for all those things that you really *love*. And that, for sure, is a must-do.

11

DANGER ZONES
Storage Areas

You're now through most of the biggest, toughest areas of the house to organize. You've sorted your clothes and become a pro with a label maker, and you can see the surface of your desk. Congratulations! Don't pop the champagne yet, though. Maybe I'm cruel, but I've saved the worst for when you're nearing the finish line. The rest of this book has been boot camp and officer training. Now you're prepared for the real war.

Yes, it's time to take a look at your long-term storage areas: attics, basements, and storage units. Rest assured that even if you don't have access to any of those—if you're an apartment dweller with no storage unit or you live in a home with no attic or basement—this chapter is still for you. Undoubtedly, you have storage somewhere in your house: a place where you pack away the things that you rarely access.

The trouble with long-term storage areas is that they enable us to be undisciplined with what we keep versus what we donate or throw away. The result is a veritable warehouse of clutter. I once heard that the architect Frank Lloyd Wright hated garages and attics for that reason. He much preferred carports to closed garages, because he felt that their openness would discourage clients from hoarding. Frank Lloyd Wright probably didn't bother himself too much with where his clients were supposed to put their lawn mowers and holiday decorations; those weren't *his* problem. I still love his philosophy in theory.

We live in a more practical world. Sometimes we have valid reasons for wanting or needing the extra space to store things that are important to us emotionally or are used less often but are necessary. Just because we have the space for storage doesn't mean we should fill it to the brim and forget about it. We should look at our storage areas the same way we do the rest of our homes: We should want them to be pleasing and practical—and navigable.

Because purging the storage area is such a big job, bear in mind that you may not be able to do the steps for the entire space all at once. You may have to start in one corner, do all the steps for that portion, and work your way through the rest in manageable chunks. Either way, the steps apply; simply tailor the order of events to your needs.

In this chapter, we'll go through the steps for the entire storage area, then focus on two particularly difficult categories of things we keep: 1) sentimental items, such as family heirlooms; and 2) children's art, schoolwork, and keepsakes. Finally, we'll talk about how to help our aging parents downsize their own storage.

The Steps for Your Storage Area

After my business was featured in the *New York Times,* a woman named Nancy wrote to me that her husband was an indiscriminate collector—

he saved everything from wine corks to more meaningful things, and it was all stuffed into boxes. As a result, their basement was full from floor to ceiling, with only narrow, snaking pathways for walking.

When things reach that level, organizing can seem completely daunting. My advice to Nancy was to designate a "basement date night" once a week until the job was done. I told her she should bring a bottle of wine for their trip down memory lane—cork saving optional.

I would give the same advice to anyone facing a similar situation. If there are two adults in your household, whether or not you both contributed to the accumulation, you should tackle the job together. Not only is it more respectful than making assumptions about what your spouse or partner might want to keep, but it also invests each half of the couple in maintaining the order. It stands to reason that you want to make the experience as pleasant as possible. Turn on some music to help keep your energy up, and keep the memories flowing.

Step 1: Purge

Rule number one is: **Your storage area is for things you use.** This rule seems so basic, yet few of us follow it. A storage area becomes the opposite: the place we put all the stuff we *don't* use. That's just silly.

There are few categories for which we need long-term storage. Let's first list those:

- **Air conditioners**
- **Ski equipment and sleds** (as long as you actually ski and sled)
- **Holiday decorations**
- **Camping equipment**
- **Summer camp trunks**
- **Gardening equipment and anything used in a shed, yard, or the car**, such as a shovel, hose, spare tires, rake, lawn mower, snow blower, etc.

- **Luggage**
- **Sentimental items** in an edited, manageable quantity. For more on how to determine what is and isn't a keeper, read the "Sentimental Items" section later in this chapter.

That's not so much, is it? So why are our storage areas so packed to the gills? Too often long-term storage becomes a delaying tactic. Rather than follow Commandment 10—make a decision and act on it—we debate, we hesitate, and we store. Multiply this process over and over, and the next thing you know your storage area looks like the warehouse at the end of *Raiders of the Lost Ark.* Let's be clear about what you can absolutely get rid of:

✂ **Anything stuffed, mounted, or preserved.** Shells that we display are pretty. What lived inside the shell, not so much. This goes for whatever was attached to that horn, tusk, hide, or skin. I will grant you that some preserved insects can be beautiful, and certain kinds of taxidermy can be real decorator items, but the thing you've stored in a box that doesn't look so hot anymore? Get rid of it.

✂ **Every report card you ever received.** Toss them unless there are one or two that are special to you for some reason—for example, because there is a personal, meaningful note written in by a favorite teacher.

✂ **Tax returns older than seven years.** Unless you're running for public office.

✂ **Old issues of *National Geographic*, etc.** If they're in a box buried in your basement, no one is reading them anyway.

Chances are, a few things have changed in the natural world since the magazines were published.

✄ **Documents such as papers from college.** Ask yourself if anyone—including you—will ever want to read them again. Remember that all documents that don't exist digitally can be scanned and saved to your hard drive.

✄ **Currently unused housewares and furniture.** These are some of the bulkiest items that people store. Our reasons for keeping a bookcase or an old electric mixer are usually one of the following: 1) What if we end up needing it because something we currently own breaks? 2) What if we buy a weekend house and we need to fill it? and 3) What if one of the children can use it in a dorm room or first apartment? To these three questions, I respond: no, no, and no. The rule of thumb for housewares and furniture is to keep only the things that are right for the life you currently lead, not the imaginary life you might lead in the future.

✄ **Collections.** Ask yourself: If I don't have room to display my collection of baseball cards/vinegar cruets/fossils, why am I keeping it? If it's worth something, then by all means get it appraised and consider displaying it more appropriately or selling it. If, like most people's, your collection consists of a lot of junk and possibly a few gems, then it would be better to display the gems and get rid of the rest.

✄ **Unused sporting equipment.** Remember, this is about the life you lead, not the one you used to lead. If people were still using wooden rackets, the last time you played tennis, it's time to say goodbye. Apply the same rule to big-ticket items such as stationary bikes—use it or sell it; don't let it guilt you from the basement.

Steps 2 and 3: Design and Organize

You wouldn't just pile stuff on the floor of your bedroom or living room, and the same should hold true for your garage, basement, attic, or storage unit. Everything should be off the floor.

Sturdy **industrial shelving** works for this purpose. In smaller areas such as storage units, **rolling carts** can come in handy, since you can roll them out in order to reach whatever is stored in back.

Here are some other tips and strategies:

- **Store like with like.** Commandment 5 is important here. Don't be tempted to store disparate items in a single container.

- **Organize containers by category.** This way you always know where to find things. Keep documents in one area, sentimental items in another.

- **Use only plastic containers.** This is particularly important in storage units, attics, and basements where you want to keep things safe from dampness. Definitely don't store anything—including documents—in brown cardboard boxes. They suck up moisture and attract infestations.

- **Utilize smart labeling.** Be as specific as possible. For example, if you have several boxes of camping equipment, one box might be labeled CAMPING—SLEEPING BAGS and another CAMPING—TENTS. If you keep multiple boxes within a particular category—such as Christmas decorations—then it's helpful to number the boxes (1 of 3, and so on). This way, when you go to your storage area to pull out all the decorations, you don't inadvertently forget one.

- **Suspend storage from the walls.** This works especially well in garages. Install wall hooks and mounts for shovels and hoses. Install shelves for antifreeze and other auto supplies. The same for gardening equipment. You might be able to add a great worktable in your garage or basement. You *might* even be able to make room for those bulky items that currently take up room in the pantry, such as water bottles, cases of seltzer, dog food, etc.

Step 4: Maintain

As in the rest of the home, the steps aren't meant to be a once-in-a-lifetime experience. You have to keep revisiting. For instance, you may think there's a good reason to keep your eleven-year-old daughter's Barbie dolls in storage in case she decides she wants to play with them again. You need to reevaluate that decision a year from now. Make it an annual habit to take a tour of your storage areas. That will keep quantities down and will also ensure that you can find the things you need. You don't want those air conditioners buried beneath a teetering pile by the time you need them next June.

Remember my admonishment when we started purging the storage area: **Storage is for things you actually use.** In my own home, this is all I store:

- summer camp gear
- ski clothes and gear

I'll tell you what I never, ever store: furniture. My theory is that it's not worth the money I'd have to spend on a storage unit to keep the stuff, and the resale value of anything but expensive furniture is pretty low. My husband teases me that my philosophy is: Toss first, ask questions later. You know what? I'm fine with that.

Sentimental Items

Of all the things we keep, sentimental items are the most difficult to purge. In the next section, we'll discuss how to make decisions about your children's artwork and schoolwork, but let's focus on the more adult items for the time being. I'm talking about all those things that you hang onto for emotional reasons and either a) can't *bear* to part with; or b) would feel too *guilty* to part with.

Sentimental is in the eye of the beholder. What may look like a rusty old Matchbox car to someone else is actually a treasured present from your favorite grandmother. Only you can decide what is deeply important to you and what you'd be heartbroken to get rid of. However, as you evaluate what to keep versus what to bid a fond farewell, consider the following:

1. **Your space constraints aren't flexible.** You have only so much room.
2. **Quality is more important than quantity.** You're far more likely to spend time with a *well-edited* collection of sentimental items. Identify those things that best symbolize a moment or person you want to remember.
3. **Do you truly love the sentimental item?**

That last bullet point is a biggie. Sometimes we keep things not because the possession means a great deal to us but because the person or the event did. These unloved items are the things that can become albatrosses around our necks. Here are some examples of what I'm talking about:

✂ **Family heirlooms that are not to your taste.** If you would never display it in your home, there is absolutely no reason to keep it. If the item is worth something, then sell it. You can put the proceeds in your children's college fund if that makes you feel better.

✂ **Boxes of papers from parents or grandparents that you don't really want or appreciate.** I understand the appeal of these things if you're tracing your family history—in which case, digitally scan everything; the papers will be much safer that way, and you can keep precious originals. But anything else, such as documents that mean nothing to you and photos of people you don't know, should be purged.

✂ **Unused wedding gifts.** Even if we don't use them and never used them, we feel somehow superstitious getting rid of them. I promise, your marriage will not end if you give them away.

✂ **Unwanted monogrammed presents.** I talked about the evils of monogramming in chapter 5, and it's no less true here. It feels so odd to give away something with our initials or some other family member's initials, as if we're dismissing the importance of the person or the occasion that the gift marked. This is your guilt talking, and it has no real basis in fact.

Finally, there are two things that should give you peace of mind as you unburden yourself of some of your stockpile:

1. **You should not be expected to maintain someone else's memories.** Unless you are an archivist by profession. Even then I'd tell you it's not your responsibility to store your grandmother's high school diploma.

2. **Things can symbolize an event and a relationship, but they aren't stand-ins for the relationship.** Getting rid of a silver service that you never used doesn't make you love the person who gave it to you any less. If it has become a burden to you and your life, then it's taking on a negative connotation that I suspect no one would want it to have, least of all the person who gave it to you.

Children's Art, Schoolwork, and Keepsakes

I have clients in New York City who pay a premium to have more than one storage unit because they can never get rid of anything. One family had an entire storage unit devoted to every piece of art their children had ever generated. The parents had stored the art in huge floppy portfolios that bulged at the seams and were impossible to stack neatly. What a mess.

Step 1: Purge

Even people who accumulate nothing else have a tendency to go crazy when it comes to their children's art and schoolwork. Part of the problem goes back to that inability to make a decision—we can't decide between three versions of the same finger painting, so we keep all of them. How could we throw away homework with that nice, shiny A on the top? What about all those keepsakes, certificates, and awards? Some of these items might be worth keeping, but the amount becomes so huge that who would ever want to comb through to make a decision? Here are a few easy guidelines for what to keep and what to toss.

KEEP

- Journals
- Creative writing assignments and anything self-revelatory
- Standout pieces of art

TOSS

- ✄ Worksheets, fill-in-the-blanks, color-in-the-lines, and all tests and math homework
- ✄ Old notebooks
- ✄ Certificates saying your child participated in an after-school class
- ✄ Weekly notes home from nursery school
- ✄ A medal that everyone got for swim class
- ✄ A trophy that was given to every member of the losing team (and everyone else in the league, for that matter)
- ✄ Any unflattering, unfocused photo that your friend sent because your child was in the picture

Okay, that last bullet point is a little hard, I admit. When your child is three, everything seems like a standout. But with a little objectivity, you can probably admit that your preschooler's latest glitter-on-glue creation isn't a major milestone. Pasta glued to paper doesn't merit keeping. Crayon scribbled on paper doesn't, either. The plaster statue from the paint-your-own-pottery place *definitely* doesn't qualify for storage. You might think I sound mean, but trust me: You'll thank me later.

You should certainly sort out repetitions. One client's son had two obsessions for a period of a few years: pigs and baseball. I told her to pick out her favorite baseball drawing and her favorite pig drawing. Then I found the Holy Grail—a drawing he'd made of pigs playing baseball. Perfect! We kept that one.

One good solution if you have a prolific artist is to keep a bulletin board in the home where current art is displayed. The one rule is that the board must be neat, with everything at right angles so it doesn't look like a layered, jumbled mess. When the bulletin board gets full, you're forced to purge before you can add more.

Another great option is to **scan or digitally photograph everything your child generates, and create a gallery of your child's artwork on the computer** that can be kept forever and forwarded to grandparents. This works especially well for those 3-D art projects and LEGO creations that no one has the room to keep intact forever and ever.

Steps 2 and 3: Design and Organize

How to store all the items that you do want to keep? It's easy. As with so many organizational tasks, part of the problem is that we make things too difficult. We keep art in one place, cards in another, school photos in yet another. That's not necessary.

I recommend that my clients purchase approximately twelve-by-fifteen-by-three-inch document boxes, or coated boxes with lids. You can choose a single color for each child. I recommend one box for birth through kindergarten and one box for every two years until sixth grade (and as needed after that). Label the boxes with your child's name and the years the box encompasses. I'm so attached to this system that I recommend my clients purchase multiple boxes at once—assuming they have the room—so that they don't risk the style and color being discontinued.

Step 4: Maintain

The benefit of the system is its simplicity. Everything goes into the one box—the nice note from Grandma, the class picture, the favorite piece of art, a clipping from the first haircut. You purge *before* you deposit items in there; you don't need to keep a greeting card without a personal message, for instance. This box should be for art, writing, and keepsakes that speak to who your child is and the most important milestones.

Lest you think the system is all about practicality, I can assure you that my children love their boxes. My daughter in particular enjoys pulling down her old boxes to sort through. I guarantee you that wouldn't happen if she had to dig through piles and piles of stuff, especially if it were socked away in a basement or storage unit.

Helping Our Parents Downsize

Many of us have older parents who are facing a move to a smaller home and the purging of their possessions. Even if your parents aren't big accumulators by nature, if they've been living in the same home for decades, there will inevitably be a backlog of stuff.

The first task in helping your parents is to walk them through the process of keeping *only* what they need in terms of furniture, housewares, and clothing, then donating the rest.

The second task is to make sure you don't become a stand-in for Goodwill. If you want an item because you have always loved it, then great, accept it from your parent gladly and with thanks. If your parent is urging something on you because she can't bear to get rid of it, then you have two choices. You can say, "Mom, I love you, but I have no room for this antique bed frame." Or, if the item is small and your parent is unlikely to go in search of it in your home, this might be one occasion when a little white lie is acceptable. What most parents want is to have someone else make the decision for them, so they don't have to feel guilty or wistful. In this case, the kinder thing might be to thank your parent, take the item off her hands, then do the selling or donating yourself.

Finally, let this experience be a lesson to you: Anything that you don't purge and organize in your own home now, you *will* eventually have to deal with or your children will have to handle for you. These situations are difficult enough without burdening the next generation.

You Have My Permission

I recently presented an organizing seminar to a corporate marketing group. One participant raised his hand and said that he'd been married for eleven years, and he and his wife had never once used the flatware that they had received as a wedding gift. Now they were moving, and he didn't want to bring it with them. But his wife felt that it was bad karma to get rid of it. This was clearly driving the poor guy nuts, so I offered to text his wife right then and there to tell her that it was okay to let it go. Sometimes people need permission to get rid of the things that are weighing them down.

I don't believe in bad karma; I do believe that the fewer things you have that you don't want, the happier you'll be. So you can take this as my blanket unreserved permission to divest yourself of your unloved stuff. Sell it or give it away, but if you don't use it or want it, don't store it!

12

SCARY, HAPPY, MERRY
Organizing for Holidays

From the end of October through the turn of the New Year, it can be hard for even the naturally organized to stay on top of things. Between the flood of candy on Halloween and the slew of party invitations at year's end, the holidays crank up life's normal chaos by a factor of ten.

Things don't have to get out of control, and you don't have to spend all of January cleaning up the messes left over from the previous year. Instead, you can spend all your free time in January going to the gym, like you promised.

As with so many of the organizational quandaries we've faced in this book, the trouble is that we make things too complicated for ourselves. We have too many decorations, too many obligations, too many presents to buy, and when we get too stressed about it all, we leave too much to the last minute. Alternatively, we start obsessing over the holidays too early, and it becomes an outsized, full-time job.

It's wonderful to enjoy the holidays. It's not wonderful to let them take over our lives to such a degree that we *forget* to enjoy them. Here's how to plan ahead, savor the happy moments, and get back to normal when everything is over. You'll notice that the steps of organization aren't rigidly outlined; nonetheless, we'll be applying them as we go along.

Halloween

Some holidays are all about the food; others are more about the decorations. Halloween is about all of the above *plus* costumes. Let's look at how to tackle each.

Costumes

Parents of young children know that the stress of deciding what to be for Halloween is *major*. I mean, this is a serious life decision our children are making. If you're lucky, then the panic sets in right around October 15. If you're unlucky, then it doesn't hit until a few days before Halloween, and you're left scrambling to pull off your son's adamant desire to transform himself into a homemade T. rex in just forty-eight hours.

It's up to you, lucky Mom, to start the countdown clock a little earlier. I recommend beginning the costume search right after the back-to-school madness dies down. A few weeks into the new school year, start talking to your children about what they want to be, and give them a deadline of October 1 for a decision, especially if they will need your help making a costume. This way you can both enjoy the process instead of fighting over it. Once your children have decided what they want to be, it's a great time to go through dress-up stashes to see if you can repurpose anything. If you're planning to purchase a costume online, leave yourself enough time to exchange it for a different size in case it doesn't fit.

Be realistic about saving costumes after the holiday. If you have a child who loves playing dress-up, add it to the collection, stored in a labeled plastic container wherever you keep the toys. However, **if there's little chance the costume will be worn again, donate it.** Definitely don't store it with the Halloween decorations—chances that the costume in question will fit one of your children, and their plans, the following year are very slim.

Halloween Decorations

I have friends who love Halloween more than any other holiday, and the decorations are a big part of that. If this describes you, then the moment to get out all your black cats, skeletons, and pumpkins is two weeks before the holiday—just enough time to enjoy them and not so long that it seems like you're running a professional haunted house. You'll weed through your decorations, getting rid of anything that's seen its best days, and you'll put everything back in a labeled container when you're done—which should be November 1. This container can be stored wherever you have the most room for items that are retrieved once a year—under the bed, on an upper shelf in a closet, or in your long-term storage area (garage, attic, or storage unit).

Candy

It's Halloween, and you're racing home from work, but first you have to dash into the drugstore to buy up whatever candy is left so you don't have to turn out the lights and pretend you're not home when the first trick-or-treater rings your bell. Sound familiar? Buy your candy early and save money. Candy prices are highest in the two weeks before Halloween.

What to do with all that Halloween candy when the holiday is over? If your children are like mine, they pull in way more than they (or you) can eat. Fill a large glass jar with candy and leave it on the kitchen counter for a few weeks of special dessert. After that, we invite some of my children's friends over and make a candy cake. Whether you bake it from scratch or from a mix, and whether you make one big cake or a bunch of cupcakes, doesn't matter. The key is that you decorate it with all that leftover candy. The children can get a spectacular sugar high, and if they don't finish it all in one sitting, send the remains home with your children's friends!

Thanksgiving and Other Feasts

Everyone celebrates Thanksgiving, and most of us will be gathering with friends or family on at least one other occasion—if not several more—throughout the holiday season. If you are always a guest and never a host, your task is easy. But if, like most of us, you end up hosting a huge dinner for more people than you entertain the rest of the year, then you need to do some planning.

Scheduling and Advance Preparations

Look at your master calendar and figure out when you'll be hosting. Get those dates marked and start assessing the head count as far in advance as possible so you can figure out what you need. A buffet dinner is easier than a sit-down, but either way you may need to bring in some supplies. Plan your menu, then evaluate the following needs and make your shopping list:

☐ **Cooking tools and specialized pans.** If that roast beef requires an instant-read meat thermometer, make sure you have one. The same thing goes for any specialized baking equipment, such as pans of a particular shape or size.

☐ **Serving dishes and utensils.** You definitely don't want to start serving dinner only to realize that you don't have a platter big enough for the main course; the same goes for serving forks and spoons. Compare your menu to your serving dishes and figure out exactly what recipes will go in what bowls and with which serving utensils.

☐ **Plates, glasses, and eating utensils.** Maybe some breakage has occurred since the last time you pulled out your wineglasses. Do your count well in advance of the holiday so you can stock up before the Thanksgiving rush. I'm a big fan of the little decorative rings you can use to help guests identify their wineglasses, especially if you don't have a huge surplus.

☐ **Seating.** If the meal is a sit-down, then count up how many chairs you'll need. Even if you plan for people to perch or stand, bear in mind your guest list. If you will have a mix of

211

older relatives, then you need to make allowances for folks who will need a stable place to sit and set their plates.

Organized Meal Serving

Refer to my advice in chapter 8 for more on streamlining in the kitchen and when entertaining. Here are some additional tips:

- **Keep it simple with appetizers.** Save your energy for the meal. A lovely cheese tray and some mixed nuts will satisfy everyone. Remember: Cooked appetizers are for caterers.

- **Don't make ten dishes if five will suffice.** You don't need three different kinds of potatoes, two different kinds of stuffing, and on and on. No one can eat that much, and the food waste can be awful to behold.

- **Avoid recipes that require last-minute steps and focused attention.** Aim for dishes that can be prepared in advance and reheated prior to the meal. You can find great recipes for make-ahead gravy, which is one of the most stressful things to throw together in the five minutes before you want to serve the meal.

- **Don't hesitate to serve prepared foods alongside the home-made.** And I forbid you to make explanations or apologies.

- **Before the first guest arrives, have everything set to serve coffee.** Measure out the coffee in the coffeemaker and fill it with water. Have an insulated carafe and a dish of sweeteners at the ready, and fill a small pitcher with cream and leave it in the refrigerator. When your guests finish dinner, push the button on the coffeemaker and sink into a chair.

Follow this advice, and if all goes well, maybe you won't be so traumatized, and you'll actually want to do the whole thing over again next year.

Gift-giving Holidays

Even the social butterflies among us can be flattened by the time we get to December. As lovely as it is to give and receive, the pressure for everything to be perfect, and for everyone to be happy is really intense. Moms feel that particularly acutely because we're usually the ones doing the planning, arranging, and shopping. Let's break it down and try to make things as easy yet pleasurable as possible.

Gift Shopping

Some of my clients love shopping. They shop all the time. I spend most of my year telling them to stop shopping so much because they already have more stuff than they can keep organized.

But at the holidays, they have me beat, because I *hate* shopping for gifts. I like shopping at other times of the year, but searching for gifts makes me cranky. I find it stressful trying to figure out what everyone might like. My main goal is to get it done as quickly and efficiently as possible.

You might not hate gift shopping as much as I do, but you can take some time-saving tips from my strong aversion. I'll be happy that my suffering has helped someone else.

- **Make a list.** Write down not just the names of everyone you need to buy for but also the items that you would like to give them. This way you can cross off names as you go and you don't risk forgetting anyone or doubling up on a gift because you forgot you've already bought a shirt for Uncle Joe.

- **Buy multiples** of a gift you love, and give it to as many people on the gift list as possible. You might not be able to give the same gift to both your sisters, but you could probably give the same gift to two people who don't know each other, or to relatives on opposite sides of the family tree.

- **Gift cards** are a gift to you. They're available in any denomination, are appropriate for any age (and as children get older and their tastes get more specific, they're really the safest bet), and they allow recipients to select the gift that they really want. Plus, you can stock up in advance and be ready for any eventuality, such as that last-minute invitation. Just be aware of the expiration dates, and either use them yourself or give them as birthday gifts in the coming months.

- **Buy as many gifts as possible online.** This is a great way of checking off items on your list in a calm environment, and if you can buy multiple gifts from one retailer, you increase the likelihood of free shipping.

- **Complimentary gift wrapping saves loads of time.** Unless wrapping gives you joy, take advantage of this free service when you buy in bricks-and-mortar stores.

- **Have hostess gifts on hand**, and keep them simple. If you usually bake something when you go to someone's house, it's okay to give yourself a break. A bottle of wine, bakery dessert, or box of chocolates can be just as nice. It's the thought that counts, right?

- **Keep track of holiday tipping.** You can make the annual ritual a lot easier if you don't have to reinvent the wheel each year. Keep a spreadsheet of all of the holiday tips you give—this way you know your budget, and you don't forget anyone. Otherwise, you may not remember how much you tipped your mail carrier last year, but guaranteed, she or he will.

Holiday Decorations

Decorations can make a home festive, but it's easy to go overboard to the point that things look and feel cluttered. I advise my clients to view their decorations with the same critical eye they would cast on anything in the home. If you look at your accumulation, it should be fairly easy to identify what you genuinely love versus what you keep because you feel you should. It's time to end this sense of obligation. Get rid of:

- ✂ **Unused menorahs.** I've been in homes with ten menorahs stashed away here and there, some that are treasured, others that don't at all suit their taste, and others that were glued together with Popsicle sticks in Hebrew school. Keep the ones you love and will use; if you'd like a keepsake, take a digital picture. You can let each child keep a favorite.

- ✂ **Deteriorating handmade ornaments.** You know the ones I mean: Maybe you made them out of construction paper one snowy December day, and now, three years later, the ornaments have started to crumble and curl. Take a digital picture if you want to remember them, but don't keep them.

✂ **Anything that was given to you by someone else but that you don't really love.** Such as that first-anniversary ornament your aunt gave you that you always hang on the back of the tree.

If the holidays are all about enjoying special times together, then you should surround yourself with meaningful items that reflect them—don't weigh yourself down with excess. Be sure to purge before you put up your decorations each year, and purge yet again when you take them down—fixing burnt-out bulbs and tossing broken ornaments. Store everything in matching plastic containers labeled with the holiday. As noted in chapter 11, if there is more than one container, number each container (CHRISTMAS 1 OF 3, for example) so that you know exactly how many to retrieve from your storage area next year.

Holiday Greetings

How many times has your Christmas card turned into a New Year's card because you couldn't get your act together in time to get it out in December? There's less reason now that digital cards are so easy to generate and email to your list, saving paper and postage. If you have older relatives who really appreciate a paper card, there are card companies that will not only allow you to design your own digital card for email but will also print and snail-mail cards to as many recipients as you like. They charge by the card, and postage is included.

If part of the reason for the delay in sending a card is that you have trouble choosing one picture from your mass of images, refer back to chapter 10 for advice on getting your photos in order and creating a "best of" folder that will make choosing a great photo a cinch. Finally, keep it simple. One great picture is perfect. No one needs to see twelve combinations of your family, lovely though they may be.

Happy Holidays

If there's one last piece of advice I would leave you with for the holiday season, it's this: Don't be a martyr. You don't have to bake for the Brownie troop, plan the office holiday party, and single-handedly cook the entire five-course holiday meal. Ask for help when you need it, and remember the lessons of saying no that we learned back in chapter 10. The holidays are meant to be enjoyed with the people we love, not rushed through in a mad race to the finish. As with organizing a closet, if we fill our lives with fewer commitments, we tend to enjoy the ones we have so much more.

Okay, I lied. I do have one other piece of advice to leave you with: Have fun!

13

LET'S TAKE THIS SHOW
ON THE ROAD
Traveling and Moving

It's time for the on-the-road test of all the skills you've learned in the rest of this book. You've graduated from organizing closets to the big time: moving.

The very thought of packing up a household, especially with young children, can trigger post-traumatic stress disorder in just about anyone who has ever done it. I'm not going to kid you into thinking that moving will ever be easy. There's a reason it's right up there with grief, divorce, and job loss as the all-time greatest sources of stress in life. But you can make the process easier on yourself and on your family. And if you do it right, then you can also improve your quality of life in the long term.

Obviously, it's a lot more fun to pack for a short trip, but there's plenty of anxiety to be found on vacation, from keeping track of the luggage to keeping track of the children. Let's look at the best ways to wrap up your household—safely and securely—and move it elsewhere, whether for a week in another country or to a new home across country. We'll start with the easy stuff first.

Organizing for Travel

When I was about fifteen, I went on a teen bus tour around the country. It involved packing for weeks of travel and not always knowing when I'd have access to a washer and dryer. Plus, we weren't in one spot larger than a few nights at a time, so we could never unpack. Despite these challenges, my suitcase was pristine the entire time. I wish I had thought to take a picture of it. Anyway, one night we were staying in tents in a campground that had a laundry room, so while the other kids dumped out their suitcases willy-nilly and promptly crashed in their sleeping bags, I dutifully took all my stuff to the laundry room and washed and folded everything, then neatly repacked it in my suitcase. That took a good long while. All the time I was safe and sound indoors, I was completely unaware that a freak wind had picked up and thrown the entire campground into disarray. When I got back to the campsite with my tidy bundle, my friends looked more bedraggled than usual, and their clothing had been blown all over the place and caked in mud. The moral to this story is: I've rarely gone wrong with packing. Until the Great Puerto Rico Disaster, that is.

The twins were under a year old, and it was December. Naturally, being who I am, I had arrived at the airport two and a half hours early for our flight to San Juan. Nonetheless, we got the unfortunate news that the airline had oversold the flight and there were no seats for us. What was more, they didn't know when their next available flight would be. After we waited around the airport for six hours (you remember the infant twins, right? Okay, good, because I want you to have a vivid picture of what those six hours entailed), they put us on a flight to Orlando, Florida. We'd be staying there overnight, and then we could fly to Puerto Rico the next day. Great!

Not great. Because, you see, we were told that our luggage had already gone to Puerto Rico on the original flight, so we landed in Orlando with nothing. It wasn't a complete disaster, I did have enough diapers and formula. And at midnight in the Orlando airport, we managed to find some Tweety Bird underwear and socks for me to sleep in and some equally ridiculous themed underwear for my husband. We figured we'd laugh about it—eventually.

The next day, we arrived in Puerto Rico looking forward to hot showers and clean clothes neatly packed by yours truly. However, our luggage, which had supposedly traveled to Puerto Rico ahead of us, wasn't waiting at the airport. And it didn't show up for *three more days.* Luckily, we were in Puerto Rico, not the middle of nowhere, so it wasn't as if I couldn't scramble and find us a few things to wear. But it was also Christmas Day, so our immediate options were limited, and who wants to spend the first few days of vacation buying necessities? And with two babies in tow? Not to mention I had to buy a bathing suit in the hotel gift shop (my husband didn't understand why that was so stressful for me, but every woman knows the pain of buying a bathing suit, never mind finding the perfect one that fits).

Lost luggage can ruin a vacation. And unless you manage to pack everything in a carry-on, there's nothing you can do to prevent it. But you can pack in such a way that you lessen the potential for disaster. I'll give you all my tried-and-true tips on how to do that, and I'll also give you my best advice for planning your trip.

Trip Planning

The best way to save money on vacation travel is to **plan ahead.** Then you can scour the airline fares and travel sites and buy at the exact moment when fares are lowest.

If you take an annual trip to the same location every year, you can start looking for deals a year in advance. For example, if you know that you spend every Thanksgiving with family in Florida, the best time to book that trip is right after Thanksgiving in the current year when you can pay easily half as much.

There's no reason not to plan your hotel accommodations far ahead as well. Remember, **hotel reservations typically can be canceled without penalty with only twenty-four hours' notice.** If you're renting a house or staying at a bed-and-breakfast, they might require as much as thirty days' notice, but you'll almost certainly know your plans by then, so there's no reason to delay.

Bear in mind that **trip insurance** is surprisingly affordable. If you're planning a big trip for your family and investing a lot of time and financial resources, it can be a worthwhile investment. That way, if plans change or someone comes down with the flu, you're covered.

Booking activities ahead of time can make a huge difference, especially when you're traveling to a top tourist destination. If you know that you want to see whales on your trip to Vancouver, then why not book seats on that cruise before you leave? The same goes for special museum exhibits—**check websites in advance and find out whether you need a separate ticket and if your spot can be reserved in advance.** This is worthwhile if you're planning to tour a top historical site during the summer or on a holiday weekend; it's awful to arrive and find a line snaking around the block. Have you checked how long the wait is for a tour of the White House? If that's number one on your list of things to do on your July 4 weekend trip to Wash-

---

TRAVEL SAFE

Here are two of my best pieces of advice for families traveling abroad. I live by these rules.

1. Remember that all family members, even babies, need passports for travel outside the US. Make copies of your passports and important documents, and keep them in a carry-on bag other than the one where you keep the originals.

2. Put a piece of hotel stationery in your children's pockets before you leave your accommodations each morning. Even older children may forget where they're staying if they get lost, particularly in a foreign country.

---

ington, DC, you should book your spots the second you know you're going. I even **make restaurant reservations in advance.** If dinner plans change at the last minute, you can always cancel, but you won't be able to get a table at a popular restaurant at the last minute.

Smart Packing

My family travels several times a year, and we've been doing that since my twins were babies, so I've figured out some handy tricks along the way. Here's my best advice.

Send heavy stuff in advance.
If you're traveling for a week or more with babies or very young children, then diapers, toiletries, sunscreen, Benadryl, and all those other necessities could easily fill all your luggage, not to mention weigh

a ton. Whenever possible, ship your toiletries (especially diapers!) to the place where you'll be staying a week in advance of your trip. There are several online drugstores that will ship for free and spare you that load in your luggage—or the risk of essential items going astray.

Bring only essential toiletries.

If you don't have the luxury of shipping ahead, then bring only the things you can't live without and in the smallest possible quantities. Opt for using the shampoo and soap that the hotel provides, or have your whole family share what you bring from home. Pare down your makeup routine to the minimum; you'll want basics that you can apply quickly. Use sample sizes when possible—I store a select assortment in a labeled box in my linen closet so they're always ready to pull out for trips—or purchase three-ounce (or less), airline-friendly plastic containers for transferring small amounts of your necessities.

Keep a bag of toiletries packed and ready to go.

For families who travel often, I recommend keeping a travel bag at home that is always stocked with your must-have items—this makes it much less likely that you'll forget something key.

Make smart use of carry-ons.

Here's what should be brought with you on the plane:

- **All prescription and over-the-counter medicines,** as well as contact lens supplies.
- **Valuables** such as jewelry and important documents.
- **One bathing suit and change of clothes** per person.
- **Special-occasion outfits.** If you're traveling to an event such as a wedding, carry on your dress, children's outfits, spouse's suit or tuxedo, and the shoes you plan to wear.

- **Electronics and chargers.** These would be expensive to replace, and you wouldn't want to be without them for even a few days. Before you leave, check that your camera works and that you have an extra battery and memory card. Make sure you have the right chargers for your phone, laptop, and children's video games. Take the right travel adaptors if you're going to a foreign country—and don't assume that the same travel adaptor works in Ireland and Spain. It doesn't.

Pack clothing using the rule of fractions.

Let's say you have four members in your family. You will pack four suitcases. Into each suitcase you will put a quarter of each person's clothing. That way, if three out of four of your bags are lost, each member of the family will have enough to wear until luggage can be located. In the spirit of full disclosure, I will tell you that my husband thinks I am completely out of my mind when I do this, and he refuses to participate. His naysaying doesn't bother me; you can apply the rule to any degree that you want. Maybe you have two children, so you split their clothing half and half between two suitcases. You can do the same for you and your husband (if your husband doesn't think you're crazy).

Pack light.

With airline fees skyrocketing, there's plenty of financial incentive for not taking your whole wardrobe on vacation. Here's a list of what I've found to be excellent wardrobe strategies:

- **Choose one color scheme** and stick to items that you can mix and match; all tops should go with all bottoms.
- **Opt for pieces that can be layered.** This offers a greater number of outfits, as well as flexibility in case of temperature changes.

- **Rely on dark jeans,** which are suitable in almost any environment and are easily dabbed clean.
- **Pack as few pairs of shoes as possible.** Think day, evening, and athletic, and that should cover you for any eventuality. I'm fond of metallic finishes, because they go with everything.
- **Have fun with accessories,** such as jewelry and scarves, which will add a pop of interest to your neutral outfits.

Utilize all the nooks and crannies in your suitcases.

Shoes can be stuffed with small bagged items, and T-shirts and articles of clothing that aren't wrinkle-prone can be rolled, which takes up less space than folding.

Plan ahead for airport delays, and pack entertainment.

Lots of parents think about stuff to do on the plane, but we forget that young children are often wound up and climbing the walls of the airport. I discovered two foolproof, easily packable ways of engaging young children and encouraging them to blow off steam before they're strapped in for a few hours: 1) a jump rope and 2) balloons. So simple. The pleasures of the jump rope are obvious. And the balloons: Blow one up, hand it to your four-year-old, and I guarantee he'll have three new friends within five minutes. P.S., that jump rope can be reused if you want to get some exercise on your trip.

Packing for Summer Camp

There's an old joke about how meticulous and careful brand-new parents are compared to parents who are on their second or third child. First time around, you sterilize everything your child might touch. By the third time around, your child and your dog are sharing the same chew toys.

The same philosophy goes for summer-camp packing. The first time your precious one goes off for weeks in the wilderness, you lovingly embroider her name onto every piece of clothing, and you cram every toiletry and technical fiber you can think of into a trunk that is so heavy, you need a crane to get it into your car. A few weeks later, your child comes home never having used her fingernail clippers and clearly having worn only the top layer of that trunk full of stuff. At that point you realize something important: **A child needs very little at camp.**

Especially if you've got newbie campers who don't know what they will and won't need, it's important to follow the packing list that their camp provides. Don't send them with *more* than that, because chances are good that those extra items will arrive home unused—or not at all. And don't be tempted to send them with over-the-counter medicines, which are forbidden by most camps—that's what the infirmary is for. In terms of toiletries, this is really all your child needs:

- ☐ toothbrush and toothpaste
- ☐ soap
- ☐ shampoo
- ☐ sunscreen in whatever delivery method they'll use—stick, spray, etc.
- ☐ mosquito repellent
- ☐ anti-itch ointment if they're bite-prone

When my twins' trunks get to camp, the counselors probably stand around and laugh at the way I pack them. Let's just say that **I'm a big fan of self-sealing plastic bags.** Everything goes in its own bag—jeans and T-shirts go in larger plastic travel bags; socks and underwear in another; bathing suits in another. My son, Matthew, likes to leave his socks and underwear that way for his entire stay because he finds that keeps things organized. (This is the same child who, when I asked him what I could bring him on visiting day, had only one request: Febreze. "Mom," he said, "some of the older boys are starting to smell.")

Packing for camp is one of those times when it's helpful to **listen to your child.** Especially if he has been to camp before—then he really does know best. Trust him when he insists that he won't wear the extra jacket that you're insisting he should bring "just in case." Bear in mind that none of my "pack light" admonitions count if you have an adolescent daughter, in which case she will insist that she needs everything from nail polish to party outfits, and there's no point in arguing with her.

Here are some other tried-and-true (and personally tested) tips for making packing and unpacking a breeze:

- Forget ironing or sewing on labels. Arm yourself with a **laundry marker,** and write the child's name inside the collar or waistband. So much easier—you will not believe the time it saves. Another option is **washable label stickers,** which I absolutely love (go to www.labeldaddy.com). These are great for children's jackets and uniforms as well—anything leaving the home that you want to come back. I'd stick them on my children if I could.

- When you're purchasing the eighteen pairs of socks and underpants required, **buy an extra dozen** of each. Have these in your children's drawers for when they return from camp. Whatever makes it home after the summer will be ripe for the trash bin.

- Separate out anything specific to camp: camp towels, linens, clothing with the camp logo, "bunk junk" (small games, flashlights, canteens). Either **store these things in the trunk that**

your child uses at camp or in a labeled plastic container. When packing next year, you'll have it all in one place.

- **Tell your child not to bring home any shoes except the ones on his/her feet.** They will just get tossed anyway. Believe me.

- **Don't send anything with your child that you would be disappointed not to get back.** Pack older clothes that are nearing their expiration date anyway.

- **Check for lice** before your child gets in the car for the trip back home. You'll thank me later.

Moving

When most people think about preparing for a move, they imagine amassing boxes and packing tape. To my mind, that is putting the cart before the horse. Before you pack a single box, your first step is to purge. You've got many tasks to tackle after that, so let's take them one by one. In this case, there are only three steps—purge, design, and organize. For advice on how to maintain in the long term, please read the rest of this book! Finally, we'll finish up with some tips for how to make moving day smoother.

Step 1: Purge

It's bad enough to store something you don't want, but packing it up and paying someone to move it is really a waste. Fill your garbage bags *before* the movers have arrived—don't pay them to move what you'll eventually donate or trash.

Maybe you've been reasonably good about purging and have already implemented a number of the systems in this book, in which case, great. Most likely, a move will force you to dig deeper into your storage areas than you ever have, and to look with an even more jaundiced eye at your accumulation of books or CDs or whatever is filling your shelves and drawers. Once you start imagining wrapping up all that stuff, it's amazing how much less attached to it you can become. The purging can start the moment you know you're planning a move in the next year, even if you haven't found your new house yet.

Step 2: Design

Use a tape measure and calculate the linear feet of storage in your current home and in the home you will be moving into, then compare the two measurements. Don't just trust your eyes. Even if the new home is bigger, that doesn't mean all of its storage spaces will be larger than what you currently have. Some spaces may turn out to be smaller or configured differently.

If you are able to design and install infrastructure in closets prior to your move, that's wonderful. A few shelves in a closet can mean the difference between unpacking right away and living out of boxes for weeks. Refer back to the closet design tips in chapters 2 and 3; remember that a single-hung closet can be transformed into a double-hung closet fairly easily. Purchase your shoe shelves in advance, along with any other flexible storage items that will make it easier to unpack your clothing. Most important, **make sure any closet system you install is flexible.** Shelves should be movable.

Even if you can't install closet systems in advance, a clear sense of what items in your home belong in which storage areas will make your packing much clearer and more effective and your unpacking smoother. For instance, if you know that the contents of your current linen closet will be divided between two areas in your new home, you can label your boxes accordingly. For more about smart labeling, read on.

Step 3: Organize

Many of my clients like the idea of having movers pack for them, thinking that will make life easier and keep their belongings safer. I advise against it. Movers are incentivized to minimize damage, which is good. However, they are also paid for their time, for the amount of packing supplies they use, and for the number of boxes they pack. You have different priorities—you want to minimize damage, but you also want to keep your costs down, and you want your unpacking to be as easy and organized as possible. While you can pay movers to unpack, they can't be expected to know where everything belongs, and chances are that things won't end up where you want them. The more packing and unpacking you do yourself, the more organized you are likely to be. If you do use movers, insist on a flat rate for the move.

First, let's outline your **basic supplies.** The moving company will estimate the number of packing boxes you'll need and will deliver those. In addition, you'll want to have:

☐ Black waterproof markers.
☐ Packing tape and dispensers. The dispensers are essential; they make closing boxes so much easier and faster, and they eliminate the need for scissors. Purchase as many dispensers as there are family members who will be packing.
☐ Newspaper for wrapping and padding.
☐ Packing paper for dishes and glasses. You could use newspaper, but white dishes will need a time-consuming scrub if they get newsprint smudges.

Here are some other pointers:

- **The earlier you start, the better.** As soon as you know you're moving, begin packing things that you don't rely on in your daily life, such as decorative items.

- **Pack like with like.** This means that only kitchen items should go in boxes for the kitchen, etc. For example, if you have spare room at the top of a kitchen box, *never* stick in a few items from the living room. Instead, stuff the remaining space with newspaper.

- **Utilize smart labeling.** Each box should be labeled with the following information: 1) where the box should go and 2) what the box contains. Be as specific as possible. REBECCA BR is too general; REBECCA BR: DESK ITEMS is perfect. This will help hugely when it's time to prioritize your unpacking and find the items you need most.

- **Hanging clothing is easy to move.** I'm a big fan of wardrobe boxes. One or two of those boxes can transfer all hanging items in one fell swoop.

- **Designate a box for each bureau drawer.** Label them accordingly (MASTER BR/DRAWER 1, etc.). Another option is to pack folded clothes in laundry or even garbage bags; just be sure to label them visibly so you don't mistake those bags for actual garbage.

The Secrets to a Smoother Moving Day

As we've already discussed, purging and packing well are two of the most important things you can do to ensure an easier move. You can also prepare your new home as much as possible in advance. Whether you're moving near or far, you can do the following:

- **Set up your essential utilities.**

- **Schedule your cable appointment** for the earliest possible date after your move when your televisions will be in place.

- **Hire a locksmith** to change the locks and make duplicate keys.

- **Hire a cleaning service** to give the home the kind of deep cleaning that's harder to do once it's filled with boxes and furniture.

If you have access to your new home even a few days before the move, here are some other incredibly helpful tasks:

- **Make sure all the built-in appliances are working.** If you purchased the home, ideally, you did this on your final walk-through, but it doesn't hurt to check again. Things happen, and it's better not to have rude surprises on moving day. Just ask my husband, who once forgot to test the washing machine in our new home and found himself responsible for doing the laundry until it was fixed.

- **Unpack one bathroom** with necessities for the family, including:
    - ☐ Towels
    - ☐ Essential toiletries

☐ Basic over-the-counter medicines, such as pain relievers
☐ Prescriptions
☐ First-aid supplies

- **Leave a bag with linens** for all of the beds; you can make the beds as soon as they're assembled on moving day.

- **Drop off a suitcase for each family member** packed with three days' worth of clothing. No matter how tumultuous the move, you know you'll find something to wear.

- **Stock a bucket of cleaning supplies.** Paper towels, spray cleaner, sponges and dish soap, dishwasher detergent, laundry detergent, as well as a broom and dustpan.

- **Unpack the basic kitchen essentials.** Coffeepot and filters, and enough dishes, glasses, mugs, and utensils for the family.

- **Stock the refrigerator.** At a minimum, make sure you have milk and cold drinks, plus some snacks.

- **Grab some takeout menus** from local restaurants for those first few nights.

The Most Important Thing

The rest of this book has been largely about organizing our stuff. And that is a big and valid concern in our lives. Our belongings are important to us, and how well we keep and store them can have direct impact on our quality of life.

The subjects of traveling and moving are about way more than transferring our stuff from one place to another, though. They're about moving *us*—our families. The proper label on the box and the well-packed carry-on are physical manifestations of our desire to keep our families safe, healthy, and intact.

So, do your best with the organizing, but most important: Count heads. If you start and end your journeys with every member of your family well and accounted for, that's truly the most important thing.

14

EASY DOES IT
Final Thoughts

Organizing is incredibly powerful. It's remarkable, the degree to which our messes can hold us back—and it's amazing how much freedom, peace of mind, and confidence we can achieve once we confront and eliminate clutter and piles.

As mothers, we can't avoid the big things that throw us for a loop—family illnesses and job stresses, ER visits and unexpected phone calls from school, refrigerator meltdowns and car breakdowns. But I would love to abolish all the needless things that make our lives as mothers—and as people—more difficult. And I truly enjoy helping my clients see the light. I've had many gratifying moments as an organizer—clients are constantly telling me that our work together has changed their lives. One of my clients had an extra bedroom in her house used for nothing other than storing papers. Piles and piles and piles. It was a massive job, but over a few months, we cleaned it, sorted it, and developed a filing system. A few months later, when she lost her passport while traveling in a foreign country, she knew exactly where she had a copy that could then be faxed to the embassy. That was a pretty big problem solved by a few filing cabinets.

I had another client whose husband wasn't outright antagonistic toward my work, but he wasn't exactly encouraging, either. For the first year I worked with his wife, he couldn't be bothered to remember my name and called me only "the organizer lady." My breakthrough with him occurred when I astutely discovered that he, too, had a "hot spot"—his books. After I categorized them and put them in an attractive, accessible place, he was ecstatic—and he learned my name.

By far, the most satisfying comments I receive are from clients who tell me that their children—particularly those with attention deficit hyperactivity disorder—are calmer, happier, and better behaved now that the clutter and chaos have been removed from their homes. That is truly potent stuff.

By now I hope you've learned some valuable tips that will help make your own life happier and easier. That last word—"easier"—is really the key, isn't it? I want you to succeed, so the last thing I want to do is to make organizing more complicated than it needs to be. That's a recipe for failure, at least for most of us. I would never tell you that organizing your home will be a piece of cake—it might involve some sweat and dust-induced sneezing along the way. But it doesn't have to be so hard.

The message I want you to take away is that you don't have to change who you are in order to live a healthier, more organized life. Your home will not transform into a catalog spread overnight. You shouldn't want it to. But you can feel more in control of your life, and you can make your home a more user-friendly, comfortable, attractive place for you, your family, and any guest you choose to allow in the front door. Notice that word, "choose," because it's important. You don't have to be an entertainer if you don't want to be, the same way you don't have to be a novelist or a pastry chef. But if you do want to host dinner parties, or write that first book, or turn out a perfect *macaron,* then I hope I've shown you how you can make your kitchen cabinets and your desk a more conducive place to pursue those dreams.

I've given you lots of specific advice. Now I'd like to leave you with a few simple mantras that bear repeating. This is the Barbara Reich philosophy boiled down to its essence. And because I believe in making things easy, I'm including some real-world applications.

Barbara's Easy-Does-It Mantras

1. **The most powerful changes are the most logical.**
Application: If your children's coat are always on the floor, lower the hooks or the rods so they can reach them.

2. **Focus on what you can change.**
Application: Don't waste time complaining about immovable objects. You probably can't change the size of your closet/bathroom/kitchen, but you can control how much stuff you put in it.

3. **Do what is most distasteful to you first.**
Application: The thing that you dread the most is the thing that affects your quality of life the most. Cross it off your list and experience instant improvement.

4. **Make a decision.**
Application: Don't store that ugly pitcher because you can't commit to getting rid of it. You know you don't want it in your life, so make the decision once and for all, and you don't have to waste any more brainpower—or storage space—on it.

5. If you don't love it and don't need it, don't buy it.
Application: The blouse isn't your color or style, but it's on sale. What do you do? Repeat after me: Walk away.

6. Let a store be a store.
Application: You do not live in a twelve-thousand-square-foot big-box store. You don't need to re-create its variety or inventory on your own shelves.

I could have included at least fifteen more mantras. I could have reminded you to keep things digital and to use the same colored hangers (oops, I guess I just did). But if the list got too long, then those mantras wouldn't seem so simple. And less is more, right? I know that if I overwhelm you with detail, you'll want to walk away, like you do from that overstuffed closet. Writing a book is like shopping, or collecting, or storing. You have to know when enough is enough.

So pull out your calendar and make an appointment with yourself to get started on your own hot spots . . . and let me know how you do!

ACKNOWLEDGMENTS

I want to begin by thanking Lisanne Biolos, who was responsible for both my first client and the start of my professional organizing business. I'm forever grateful to you for seeing my potential!

Thank you to all of the amazing moms who have become clients and friends. I especially want to thank my earliest clients, Keri Bernstein, Amy Feinblatt, Lauren Geller, Jill Heller, and Erica Keswin for all of the glowing word-of-mouth recommendations and referrals you've sent my way over the years.

Thank you to Sara Berman, who told a reporter at the *New York Times* to call me in the fall of 2010. A very special thank-you to Elissa Gootman, the *New York Times* reporter who trailed me for two months, meeting my clients and watching me work. The resulting article, "Organize This," generated more buzz than I ever could have imagined and ultimately paved the way for this book.

Thank you to Dina Bakst, Marsha Bernstein, Keith Brickman, Valerie Feigen, Susan Hitzig and Ken Yaffee, Leigh Hrazdira, Jennifer Keil, Dana Kirshenbaum, and Roxanne Palin for helping make the *New York Times* story come alive.

Thank you to my managers, Perri Kipperman and David Stern, for your help and advice in every aspect of my career.

Acknowledgments

A special thank-you to Richard Abate, my literary agent; Peternelle van Arsdale, my cowriter; and my team at Atria Books: Judith Curr, Ariele Fredman, Isolde Sauer, Julia Scribner, and my editor, Amy Tannenbaum. The entire process from book proposal to book could not have been easier. You are all amazingly talented and efficient.

And finally, thank you to my mother and father, who taught me to be organized; to my beautiful children, Rebecca and Matthew, who light up my life; and to my fabulous husband, Jeff, who has supported me every step of the way. I love you all!